IN FOCUS

COLOMBIA

A Guide to the People, Politics and Culture

Colin Harding

The Latin America Bureau is an independent research and publishing organisation. It works to broaden public understanding of issues of human rights and social and economic justice in Latin America and the Caribbean.

First published in the UK in 1995 by Latin America Bureau (Research and Action) Ltd, 1 Amwell Street, London EC1R 1UL

© 1996 Colin Harding

A CIP catalogue record for this book is available from the British Library

ISBN 1 899365 X

Editing: James Ferguson

Cover photograph: first communion, Paul Smith

Cover design: Andy Dark

Design: Liz Morrell & Antonella Bianchi

Cartography: Department of Geography, University College London

Print: South Sea International Press

Trade distribution in the UK: Central Books, 99 Wallis Road, London E9 5LN

Distribution in North America: Monthly Review Press, 122 West 27th Street, New York, NY 10001

Already published in the *In Focus* series:

Jamaica (1993)
Bolivia (1994)
Venezuela (1994)
Cuba (1995)

CONTENTS

Andrés Escobar, killed for an own goal (AP)

INTRODUCTION

When Colombia's presidential elections coincided with the country's participation in the finals of the football World Cup in June 1994, government publicists regarded it as a perfect opportunity to project a new, more positive image to the world. Here was a chance to draw attention to the political and economic progress made in recent years and show what a modern, fast-growing, democratic nation Colombia had become.

But the high hopes were followed by cruel disappointment, as it all went horribly wrong. The relatively peaceful, honest and efficient elections were overshadowed by scandal and violence in both sport and politics. The winning presidential candidate, Ernesto Samper Pizano, of the dominant Liberal Party, was accused within days of the polls closing of accepting money from the Cali cocaine cartel to finance his campaign. He was obliged to issue indignant denials and to hurry off to Washington to explain himself to a sceptical Clinton administration.

A year later these allegations were still haunting the new president. Jesse Helms, the ultra-conservative chairman of the Senate Foreign Relations Committee, claimed to have testimony from a defector from the Cali cartel that Samper had accepted a suitcase full of money in return for opposing the inclusion of an extradition clause when a new constitution was being drafted in 1990. He called for tough, direct action by the US if the Colombian authorities failed to take decisive action against the drug barons.

They did just that on 9 June 1995, when Gilberto Rodríguez Orejuela, reputed to be the ultimate boss of the Cali cartel, was arrested in a safe house in the city. A few days later the organisation's 'military commander', Henry Loaiza, surrendered at an army barracks in Bogotá. Samper and his defence minister proclaimed the beginning of the end of the Cali cartel.

Congratulations poured in from around the world. But within weeks it had all gone sour again. Samper's former campaign treasurer was arrested and produced detailed evidence that the president has known about cartel contributions to his election funds. Soon afterwards the former campaign director, and current defence minister, was also detained. The Samper administration was fighting for its life.

It had been a similar story of premature celebrations at the 1994 World Cup. The strongly-fancied Colombian team was ignominiously eliminated in the preliminary round of the finals, amidst suspicions of pressure from drug and gambling interests. And no sooner had the squad arrived sheepishly back home than one of its members, Andrés Escobar, was murdered in obscure circumstances outside a Medellín nightclub. He had been unfortunate enough to score the own goal that sealed his team's fate.

It was all so sleazy, so predictable. Anybody wanting confirmation that Colombia was a corrupt and violent society, run by gangsters and racketeers, needed to look no further. These two episodes encapsulated all the negative elements of Colombia's international image: drugs, casual violence, cynical and corrupt politics.

But that is not the whole story. It is impossible to write about Colombia without facing these unpalatable aspects of the country, but to focus on the seamy side alone would be like describing modern Britain or the US with reference only to inner-city crack dealing and kids sleeping rough in the streets of big cities.

Colombia is a complex and contradictory country, with many features – not all of them negative – that set it apart from the rest of Latin America. It is both lawless and legalistic, chaotic and coherent, with a well-developed civil society and institutions. It has often appeared to teeter on the brink of disaster, but nevertheless has somehow managed to stagger on, with its basic structures apparently intact despite successive setbacks. Its government is both remarkably well-run in some respects and woefully lacking, even totally absent, in others. There a few other places in the world where the struggle between good and evil is more starkly engaged.

The more positive characteristics of this strange society at least give it some elements of hope for the future. It has a strong and diversified economy, run by competent and honest technocrats. It has enormous potential, particularly in energy: oil, gas and coal. Above all, it has a large, hard-working and endlessly resilient population. It deserves a better future.

1   LANDSCAPES AND PEOPLE: MANY COUNTRIES IN ONE

If ever a country's geography reflected and conditioned its society and politics it is Colombia's. The Andean range splits into three near the Ecuadorean frontier to the south, after marching monolithically up the west coast of South America for thousands of miles from the icy wastes of southern Chile. Any cross-country journey in central Colombia, where most of its 34 million people live, involves a succession of climbs and descents that are impressive and exhausting in equal measures.

A bus journey from the capital, Bogotá, to the big industrial city of Cali in the hot valley of the Cauca river 280km away to the south-west takes you first across the flat green expanse of the Sabana de Bogotá, the lush, mountain-girt basin that surrounds the capital on three sides. This is followed by a climb over the mountains ringing the city, a descent into the hot Magdalena valley at Girardot, an ascent to the Quindío pass (3,350m above sea level) over the Cordillera Central, the middle of three Andean spurs, a winding descent through the coffee-growing mountains around Armenia and finally a long run through the baking sugar-cane fields that gave Cali its original *raison d'être*.

Geography made Colombia more like a collection of city-states than a unitary country until quite recently. Regionalism has always been a powerful force in Colombian life, and it lingers on in the psychology of the people. This is particularly so in Medellín, the second city, high up (1,480m) in a valley surrounded by the mountains of Antioquia almost 500km to the north-west of the capital. The city's two and a half million people regard themselves almost as a race apart and are resentful of what they regard as the overweening arrogance of the distant capital. Medellín, like São Paulo in Brazil or Guayaquil in Ecuador, likes to regard itself as the real heart of the country, where wealth is generated and talent is nurtured, only to be appropriated by the undeserving bureaucrats and politicians of Bogotá.

Medellín was founded in 1616, but its wild hinterland was not properly settled, cleared and brought into cultivation until the early nineteenth century. Until then it had been a centre of gold production, some mined and some dredged from the rivers.

River and Coast   The rugged geography meant that for centuries communications between the capital and the outside world were largely confined to river transport, which was slow and hazardous. Bogotá, the highland capital, founded by Gonzalo Jiménez de Quesada in 1538, was linked to the mother country, Spain, via the Magdalena river, which, with its tributary the Cauca, runs from south to north through the heart of the country. This was the route

The Cauca valley   (Paul Smith)

taken by the produce of the hinterland, and it was also the route of the last journey of General Simón Bolívar, the Liberator, so memorably described by Gabriel García Márquez, Colombia's Nobel Prize-winning novelist, in *The General in his Labyrinth*.

The Magdalena valley towns are among the oldest in Colombia: Mompós, founded in 1537, hardly seems to have changed since then. These places had their heyday when imports from Spain were ferried up the river to Bogotá from Cartagena, and later when great rear-wheeled paddle steamers plied this river of shifting sandbanks and tricky currents. Now the unlovely oil-refining town of Barrancabermeja is the main centre for the economically important and chronically violent region known as the Magdalena Medio.

The Caribbean coast is very different from the highlands: hot, with very little variation in temperature. The people, too, are more 'tropical' than the gloomy highlanders, the *cachacos*. The main port, Cartagena, founded in 1533, was where the Spanish colonial power erected the most impressive fortifications of the entire Spanish Main, to protect its magnificent harbour. They stand to this day. This was the port from which gold, the main product of colonial New Granada, was exported to Spain. Cartagena's wealth made it an inviting target for foreign marauders, such as Sir Francis Drake, who sacked the city in 1586.

Cartagena is now being developed as a tourist resort, with a row of modern hotels stretched out along Bocagrande beach outside the town. Barranquilla, further along the coast by the mouth of the Magdalena, is now much bigger, dirtier and more industrialised. For a while both were overshadowed by Santa Marta, during the *marimba* (marijuana) boom of the 1960s and early 1970s, when the traffickers developed their own beach resort at Rodadero. Santa Marta is Colombia's oldest Spanish city, founded in 1526, as the conquerors sought to establish footholds on the Caribbean coast. Its strategic location at the foot of the Sierra Nevada de Santa Marta, the isolated clump of towering mountains where much of the weed was grown, briefly gave it the edge and excitement of a gold-rush town.

The Islands

Far out to sea are the Colombian islands of San Andrés and Providencia, more than 1,700km from Bogotá and a lot closer to the Atlantic coast of Nicaragua than to the Colombian mainland, 700km away. These islands were finally confirmed as Colombian territories under the Bárcenas-Esguerra Treaty of 1928, along with a collection of smaller islands, cays and reefs, and there are still occasional diplomatic incidents between the two countries.

Like the islands and cays of Nicaragua's Miskito coast, the population of San Andrés and Providencia, which totals about 50,000, is largely black and English-speaking, some the descendants of English Puritan settlers, pirates and African slaves. There has been a big influx of mainlanders in recent years and the racial mix is changing, particularly on San Andrés. But earlier attempts to replace the English language and Protestant (especially Baptist) religions with Spanish and Catholicism have been dropped.

San Andrés was declared a freeport in 1968, in an attempt to compete with islands such as Curaçao and Aruba, and has become a centre of sun-and-shopping tourism for Colombians keen to stock up on duty-free electronic equipment. Many of the recent hotel and resort developments have the ostentatious vulgarity that only drug money can impart, and the US has become increasingly concerned about the role of the islands as platforms for trans-shipment of cocaine to Mexico and the US.

Providencia is different: smaller (4,500 people), less developed, and with a local council and civic movement determined to save it from the excesses of neighbouring San Andrés.

Frontiers, Plains and Jungles

Back on the mainland, the country's other great regional urban centres are Bucaramanga and Cúcuta, capitals of Santander and Norte de Santander departments respectively. These are the main economic and political centres for eastern Colombia and for exchanges with Venezuela. Cúcuta, on the frontier, is a smugglers' bazaar to compare with Ciudad del Este in Paraguay.

Outside the central region and the Caribbean coast, the country remained largely unsettled until recently, when oil and drugs lured the brave or desperate to try their luck in the southern plains and jungles. Colombia still has more wild frontiers than most countries. Even large parts of the Caribbean coast were for centuries only intermittently in contact with the outside world, whose influences had a way of being absorbed and stifled - as García Márquez suggests in his masterpiece, *One Hundred Years of Solitude*, a work that should be read as more realist than magical.

Internal frontiers are still everywhere in Colombia. One of the wilder sorts is the Urabá region, on the Caribbean coast, a world away from the beaches of Cartagena and Santa Marta. It is politically part of Antioquia, but nothing could be further from the permanent spring of Medellín (which is how the tourist brochures describe it) than the sweltering lowlands of the Gulf of Urabá, which are Colombia's main banana-producing region. This is big business: Colombia has the largest Latin American quota for selling bananas to the European Union. The poor, unemployed and landless have poured down to Urabá from the highlands for decades, carving out plots of land for subsistence farming on the unsettled frontier, or finding work on the big plantations.

It is one of the most lawless and dangerous parts of the entire country, with a bewildering array of armed and paramilitary groups of all persuasions struggling for supremacy in the streets and shanty towns of Turbo, Apartadó and the other banana towns. The body count is always high here.

The jungles and mangrove swamps of the Chocó region, up by the Panamanian frontier, are remote and cut off to this day, with few roads and most transport by river and sea. Indeed, the entire Pacific coast is a backward and neglected region. The hot, humid port of Buenaventura (founded 1540) is a notoriously ill-favoured spot, even though it has a busy harbour and there is a paved road over the Western Cordillera to Cali, 145km away.

When cholera swept through parts of South America in 1991, Colombia's only serious outbreaks were in the poverty-stricken towns and villages of the Pacific seaboard, where the rickety wooden houses built on stilts over tidal inlets and the primitive public hygiene provided fertile breeding grounds for the *vibrio cholerae* bacterium. Public health schemes have been attempted in recent years, but this is also one of the worst regions for the deadly cerebral malaria and for other tropical diseases such as *uta* and leishmaniasis.

More than half of Colombia's national territory is occupied by low-lying plains and grasslands, known generically as the *llanos*, which begin not far south and east of Bogotá and stretch for hundreds of miles across the Orinoco basin into Venezuela and south until they merge into the jungles of the Amazon system, the Vaupés and Caquetá and Putumayo, with their sparse populations of tribal Indians. This whole vast area is a happy hunting ground for guerrillas and drug traffickers. Most of the cocaine processing laboratories these days are hidden away in the jungles and forests of Caquetá and Putumayo.

The llanos   *(Tony Morrison/South American Pictures)*

The *llanos*, interminable rolling grasslands that bake in the dry season and flood during the rains, constitute one of the world's largest remaining frontiers. The skilled horsemen of the *llanos* provided much of the irregular cavalry for both sides in the wars of independence in both Colombia and Venezuela. The Colombian *llanos* are still a battleground, but now the struggle is between oil companies and guerrilla columns, and between the security forces and drug-traffickers.

The region known as the *piedemonte llanero*, the foothills of Casanare and Arauca departments, are Colombia's main oil-producing regions. A pipeline carries crude from the Caño Limón field in Arauca to Coveñas on the Caribbean coast. It is a favourite target of one of the Colombia's two main guerrilla organisations, the Ejército de Liberación Nacional (National Liberation Army or ELN), which has blown up sections of the pipeline hundreds of times over the past decade, with the loss of more than 1 million barrels of oil.

Despite these security problems, Casanare promises to become an oil-boom region over the next few years. The adjacent Cusiana and Cupiagua fields have proven reserves of 2-3 billion barrels and should be producing more than 500,000 barrels per day before the end of the century. For the moment it is still wild country, with no large towns, just a string of fortified drilling camps garrisoned by units of the Colombian army's counter-insurgency forces.

Colombia has extensive jungle territory in Caquetá and Putumayo departments, along its southern frontiers with Ecuador and Peru, but the country's only outlet to the Amazon proper is a small polygon of territory centring on the busy river port of Leticia, which faces both Brazil and Peru on the other side of the great river. All these frontiers are highly porous, particularly for drugs. It is possible to walk into Brazil unhindered from Leticia into the garrison town of Tabatinga.

Bogotá

That just leaves Bogotá, the capital. It is huge (about six million people), ugly, overcrowded and chaotic. It has been acting as a magnet for migrants from the countryside for decades and has grown uncontrollably in both population and extension. Environmentally, the consequences have been dire.

Bogotá is situated on the very edge of the Sabana, 2,650m up at the foot of a range of steep, green mountains. The oldest parts of the city, Santa Fe and La Candelaria, founded in 1538, are here. Some cobbled streets of attractive, whitewashed houses have been carefully preserved, but the commercial focus of the city has shifter northwards, to Chapinero and beyond.

Further up the slopes, in the outcrops and ravines, the shanty towns of the capital have sprawled haphazardly, destroying the tree cover, fouling the watercourses and helping to turn the Bogotá river, which meanders across the Sabana until it drops down towards the Magdalena at the Tequendama falls, into one of the most polluted stretches of water in the world. The shanty towns also stretch endlessly across the Sabana to the south and the urban-industrial sprawl threatens to engulf the international airport of El Dorado to the west.

Antanas Mockus

When in October 1994 Antanas Mockus was elected mayor of Santa Fe de Bogotá - reputed to be the second most important elected post in the country - his triumph was hailed as a victory for 'anti-politics'. He was certainly not a typical Colombian politician; indeed, not a politician at all.

Mockus, the 42-year-old son of Lithuanian immigrants, is a mathematician turned philosopher who was the youngest ever rector of the National University in Bogotá. In that role he was credited with being an effective if eccentric administrator, who liked to attend meetings brandishing colourful toy swords and climbing in and out of dustbins to make some point or other that often eluded his baffled colleagues and students. His notoriety took on national proportions when at a mass meeting in the university auditorium he became so exasperated with hecklers that he turned his back on his audience and dropped his trousers. Unfortunately - or perhaps fortunately, as things have turned out - somebody in the audience had a video camera to hand and the tape of Mockus's rectoral mooning exercise found its way on to the national TV news programmes that evening.

Mockus had to resign, but his outlandish action had turned him into a national figure, and his name began to be mentioned as a possible future education minister. He showed absolutely no interest in becoming a politician, and when he was prevailed upon to stand for the mayorship of the capital, it was expressly as a 'non-political' figure. He caught the public mood and was elected by a landslide (65 per cent of the votes cast).

Many voters had come to feel that the capital was ungovernable: a dirty, overcrowded, noisy, horrendously polluted jumble of old buses, clogged traffic, uncollected rubbish and street vendors, surrounded by lawless shanty towns where about 75 per cent of the population live.

It is too soon to judge how effective he will prove - he has already launched successful experiments with street theatre to encourage drivers to respect zebra crossings and traffic lights - or to conclude if he really is part of a wave of public rejection of traditional politics and politicians. But Mockus is merely the most striking of a number of non-party figures elected in 1994 to run Cali, Cartagena, Barranquilla and other big cities.

Despite its many drawbacks, not least of which is a seemingly perpetually overcast sky, Bogotá remains, as it has been for centuries, the political and cultural centre of the country. Here are all the government departments, the biggest newspapers and magazines, the most prestigious universities, the best theatres and bookshops, the wonderful Gold Museum. The capital is the focus of most intellectual and artistic endeavours.

Bogotá's café society, the *tertulias*, used to be famous throughout the Spanish-speaking world, enabling it to lay claim to the title 'the Athens of the South', where writers and artists set the world to rights over endless cups of coffee in the salons of Carrera 7, and congressmen were given to reading from their latest collections of poetry during debates in the neo-classical National Capitol building.

It is different now. The transformation of the highland political and administrative centre into a huge, grimy industrial city began the change; the habit of competing drug gangs of settling their differences in the restaurants and night spots of the capital in the 1970s helped it along and the more recent residential and commercial migration to the suburbs have completed it.

Indigenous Colombia

Colombia is overwhelmingly *mestizo* or ethnically mixed (including Antioquia which thinks of itself as white); the Muiscas, Taironas and other indigenous peoples living in what is now Colombia at the time of the Conquest declined dramatically through a combination of war, disease, ill-treatment and intermarriage. Though some had highly-developed material cultures, they were neither as numerous nor as socially advanced as the peoples of the Aztec and Inca empires. The only substantial remaining groups of highland Indians are found in the region of Cauca and Nariño, south of Cali, where the Páez and Guambiano Indians have their reservations. This is an area of backward *haciendas* and patchworks of small farms and mountain towns of whitewashed walls and red-tiled roofs: the only part of Colombia similar in character and appearance to the Andean regions of Ecuador, Peru and Bolivia, further south, with their much larger Indian populations.

This otherness is at its most emphatic in Pasto, capital of Nariño, which sided with the Spanish during the wars of independence and then tried to join Ecuador when the post-war Gran Colombia federation broke up in 1830. It is also acknowledged in the popular image of the *pastuso*, the native of Pasto, who to other Colombians is proverbially stupid.

Other notable Indian regions are the Sierra Nevada de Santa Marta, the scene of some of the most brutal confrontations between the traditional and modern aspects of Colombian society, and the arid Guajira peninsula. *Mestizo* settlers and drug-traffickers, spurred by a mixture of land-hunger and greed, have been disputing control of the Sierra Nevada with the Kogi and Ika Indians for decades.

There are still some 60,000 Guajiro (Wayuu) Indians, who make a hard living from their flat, sweltering peninsula on the Venezuelan frontier, where smuggling and the new open-cast coalmine at El Cerrejón are the only games in town. The Guajiros, who traditionally herd sheep and goats and dig salt, have shunned many of these developments and have kept to themselves.

Afro-Colombia

Most of Colombia's black population, who make up about 18 per cent of the total, are found along the Pacific and Caribbean coasts. Many were originally brought in from Africa to work the mines of the Pacific littoral that made the beautiful southern highland city of Popayán large and prosperous in the colonial period, before it was superseded as a regional centre by Cali in the mid-nineteenth century. An estimated one million black slaves passed through the port of Cartagena until the abolition of slavery in 1851. Many escaped from the mines and sugar plantations and formed free communities of *cimarrones* in the Cauca valley and on the isolated coast.

The separate identity and equal rights of their descendants are affirmed in the 1991 constitution and subsequent legislation, but black leaders remain sceptical that ingrained discrimination and disadvantage will be easily rooted out of Colombian society. Anthropologist Jaime Arocha Rodríguez of the National University in Bogotá estimates that 10 per cent of the Colombian population are black and as many as 30 per cent are influenced by Afro-American culture (compared with two per cent indigenous Indians).

Guambiano family   *Tony Morrison/South American Pictures*

European Migration

Independent Colombia has never been a country of large-scale European immigration, like Argentina in the late nineteenth century or Venezuela since the Second World War. The *antioqueño* colonisation that produced the modern coffee economy was given additional impulse by arrivals from Spain (particularly the Basque country), but many of the colonists were natives of Medellín who moved out in search of land to clear and cultivate.

Individual immigrant families from northern Europe have achieved prominence in various fields, such as the de Greiffs (from Sweden) and the Eders (from Germany) and Bogotá Mayor Antanas Mockus was born in the capital because his parents arrived there as part of the United Nations resettlement programme for victims of the Second World War.

The other substantial immigrant group is from the Middle East, known collectively in Colombia as *turcos*. They are found everywhere, but particularly on the Caribbean coast. During the presidency of Julio César Turbay Ayala (1978-82), the 'emerging class' of *nouveaux riches* associated with the marijuana boom included many *turcos*. Turbay is itself a *turco* name, and is ubiquitous in Colombian politics: the current comptroller-general is a Turbay, as was the 1946 Liberal presidential candidate.

2   HISTORY AND POLITICS: WAR AND PEACE

The republic of Colombia was born in violence. Colombians (and Venezuelans) made up the majority of the armies that liberated first their own countries and then Ecuador, Peru and Bolivia in the course of a protracted and bloody struggle with the Spanish Crown's forces, headed by a viceroy based in Bogotá since 1739.

It was also the scene of the first continental integration project; Simón Bolívar, the Venezuelan-born Liberator of much of the Spanish empire, envisaged present-day Colombia as the centre of a Greater Colombia, a unified state comprising all the former Spanish dominions from Guayana in the east to the borders of the Viceroyalty of Peru to the south.

It worked for a while, until 1830. But by that time Bolívar had gone off to die in lonely disillusionment near Santa Marta, on his way to a European exile that was never to be. The fractious leaders of the independence struggle in Bogotá, Caracas and Quito did not share his grand vision, and their squabbling caused the disintegration of Greater Colombia.

The independence wars did not make much difference to the social structure, where the small, white (or whitish) local-born upper class continued to dominate a mass of *mestizo* labourers, artisans, ranch-hands and peasant farmers. As with its neighbours, much of Colombia's nineteenth-century history consisted of regional and power-group struggles for supremacy, under the broad heading of centralism versus federalism, in which local leaders regularly marched on Bogotá with their followers, from Cali, from the *llanos* and from the east. The remote and isolated highland capital was always the ultimate prize and worth fighting for.

Two-Party Politics   Disputes over the nature of government and territorial organisation took years to settle; the first national government, set up in 1811, was a loose federation known as the United Provinces of New Granada. The first civil war culminated in 1814 in the capture of a separatist Bogotá by United Provinces troops. From the 1840s onwards, conflict, whether through the ballot box or by force of arms, was largely between two political parties, the Liberals and Conservatives. They established themselves remarkably early in the country's independent life as institutional vehicles for local and class rivalries, and became effective means of mobilising mass participation in politics that sometimes spilt over into armed conflict.

The military interventionism that plagued almost every other Latin American republic until comparatively recently has never affected Colombia, despite the habitually high levels of political violence. The armed forces, with few exceptions, have accepted a limited but important role within the

political framework and have mostly kept out of national politics in return for considerable autonomy. There have only been two successful military uprisings since Independence: a coup and short-lived military dictatorship in 1853 and another exactly a century later.

The two great parties were (and still are) multi-class organisations, both dominated by local politicians, whether merchants, professionals or landowners; they recruit their support from the lower orders in the cities, on coffee farms and cattle ranches. In many areas during the latter half of the nineteenth century these bosses delivered their retainers to the polling stations on election day, and made sure they voted the right way. If that failed, there was always the ultimate resort to arms.

In general terms, the Liberals were the party of modernisation: free trade, the professions, competition, secularism and federalism. They dominated government for 35 years until 1885, during which time they sought to break with the colonial, closed, clerical past and integrate Colombia into an expanding world economy which revolved around the industrialising North Atlantic countries and their insatiable demand for raw materials and food.

The Conservatives represented the landed interest, were closely tied to the Catholic church, and were authoritarian, centralising and patrician in outlook. The Liberals derisively dubbed them *godos*, the embodiment of obscurantism, while the Conservatives regarded their opponents as Jacobins, freemasons and opponents of the divinely ordained order. But there were many apparent contradictions: the Medellín industrial class, for instance, the epitome of modernity, was and remains predominandtly Conservative. Party affiliation tended to be strongly regional and family-based, particularly in the countryside, and had little to do with simple class interests.

It looked rough but it worked. The two-party system, punctuated by regular and more-or-less peaceful elections and changes of party, has given the country some stability for surprisingly long periods and is still going strong.

The mid-century years were a period of liberal reform, beginning with the election of President José Hilario López in 1849. As elsewhere, legal protection of Indian communities was abolished, along with black slavery; blacks have been overwhelmingly Liberal in their sympathies ever since. Church and state were formally separated, most church property expropriated and universal male suffrage adopted in the 1853 constitution, which also provided for the direct election of provincial governors and even supreme court judges.

The 1863 constitution, which changed the country's name to United States of Colombia, was an extreme example of federalism, which even allowed the states to issue their own stamps and pass their own electoral laws. The experiment proved short-lived: there was another civil war in 1876, and when Rafael Núñez was elected president in 1880 he sided with the Conservatives to introduce a strongly centralist constitution in 1886, which remained in force until 1991. He also wrote the words for Colombia's national anthem (it had not had one until then) and made peace with the Vatican, which had excommunicated one of his Liberal predecessors.

Out went the election of state governors, to be replaced by the appointment of governors of 'departments' (as they were henceforth to be known) by the president. These arrangements gave the party in power overwhelming control of every detail of national political life, and meant the total exclusion of the other party. Núñez, regarded by many Liberals as a traitor, opened the door to a long period of Conservative rule, which lasted until 1930.

The result was the disastrous War of the Thousand Days (1899-1902), in which an unsuccessful Liberal attempt to dislodge the Conservatives degenerated into banditry and rural violence, particularly in the new coffee-growing areas of Tolima and Caldas, thereby foreshadowing *La Violencia* forty years later. Total casualties of the three-year conflict were estimated at 100,000 out of a population of about four million.

An indirect result of the civil war was the creation of the republic of Panama. Until then Panama had been a province of Colombia, albeit inaccessible by land from the rest of the country and with a long-established separatist tradition. It saw its future more as a transit area for inter-oceanic trade than as a remote outpost and was keen to see a canal built between the Atlantic and Pacific. When the Colombian senate rejected a treaty with the US for the construction of such a canal, Panama promptly seceded in November 1903 and a flat-broke government in Bogotá could do nothing about it. The US, which was to have control in perpetuity of a strip of land on either side of the canal, recognised the new republic with indecent haste.

Much chastened, the rival political parties renounced violence as a way of settling their differences for the next four decades, which were a period of relative peace. Until 1930 the Conservative Party held power without interruption, but the principle of minority representation in government at all levels was re-established, and General Rafael Reyes, who took office as president in 1904, appointed two Liberals to his five-man cabinet. This principle was later written into the constitution, in 1910. Reyes also took steps to convert the victorious Conservative forces into a professional, non-partisan army.

Although the Conservatives remained in power until 1930, the deferential, church-dominated social order that enabled them to retain their supremacy for so long was already crumbling by the start of the twentieth century. The Liberals had begun to talk of social reform, as socialist and anarchist ideas began to spread among the incipient working class. But the Conservatives did not concern themselves much with such matters; most Colombians were still illiterate after almost 50 years of their rule, and average life expectancy in 1930 was 34 years.

Populism and Reform Colombia coped quite well with the Depression, which caused neither revolution nor a serious foreign debt crisis. The inter-war period saw the Liberals, who returned to power in 1930, striving to recruit working-class supporters from the factories of Medellín and Bogotá, weaning them away from the class-based parties that had arrived with Spanish immigrants to Antioquia and developed in the new industrial suburbs. The Liberals introduced eight-hour-day legislation and encouraged the formation of trade unions.

President Alfonso López Pumarejo's 'Revolution on the March' (1934-38) was an attempt to pre-empt labour militancy, polarising society between supporters and opponents of social reform as never before and arousing unrealistic expectations. He brought in Colombia's first agrarian reform law in 1936, designed to encourage landowners to make efficient use of their properties or lose them to tenants or squatters. The state's interventionist role in the economy - the very antithesis of old-fashioned liberalism - largely dates from López's constitutional amendments of 1936.

López was followed by a more moderate Liberal, Eduardo Santos, the wealthy publisher of Bogotá's leading daily newspaper, *El Tiempo*, who disowned his predecessor's more radical measures. Internal dissension grew in the Liberal Party. A left-wing faction lost patience with piecemeal reformism and began to demand more populist measures to break the domination of the Liberal-Conservative ascendancy. They grouped around Jorge Eliécer Gaitán, a Liberal politician from a lower middle-class Bogotá background who first rose to prominence as a congressman for his attacks on the government's crude handling of a 1928 banana workers' strike at Ciénaga on the Caribbean coast, in which many died when the army opened fire on workers and their families.

Gaitán was a spellbinding orator whose rabble-rousing attacks on the ruling 'oligarchy' dismayed the party hierarchy. Carried along by mass adulation, he helped to end the era of Liberal supremacy by standing as an independent against the official party candidate in the 1946 elections, having failed to secure the nomination.

The Liberal vote split down the middle and allowed the Conservatives back into the presidential palace for the first time since 1930, even though they obtained fewer votes than the Liberals. The new president was Mariano Ospina Pérez, son and grandson of previous Conservative presidents and a far less menacing figure than the party's real leader, Laureano Gómez, an outspoken critic of representative democracy whom Liberals regarded as a neo-fascist.

Ospina tried to restrain extremist elements in the Conservative Party, who wanted revenge for the perceived outrages committed by Liberals during their 16 years of rule. But he was powerless to stem the rising tide of political violence, which came to a head on 9 April 1948, when Gaitán was assassinated, shot down in a Bogotá street. By that time he had become the unchallenged leader of the Liberal Party, despite the distrust of most of the party establishment.

The assassin was killed by enraged *gaitanistas*, and his motives remain a mystery to this day. Conservatives tend to believe in a plot by left-wingers intent on overthrowing the government in a wave of disorder, while Liberals prefer to see a Conservative conspiracy to eliminate the certain winner of the next election. Whatever the motive, the *gaitanista* mob went wild, setting off an 11-day orgy of looting, pillaging and killing in the capital and other cities that later became known as the *Bogotazo*. President Ospina called in the army to restore order in the capital, and the military eventually managed to quell the rampaging Liberal crowds, who had been left leaderless by the party's vacillating bureaucracy.

Thus began a nightmare period of communal violence, known to Colombians simply as *La Violencia*, as though it were a natural phenomenon, beyond the powers of human beings to comprehend or control. The far more sectarian Laureano Gómez took over the presidency from Mariano

Aftermath of the *Bogotazo*

Ospina in 1950 after being elected unopposed; the Liberals boycotted the polls, claiming that their lives were in danger. It was during Gómez's presidency (1950-53) that the violence really took hold, spreading across the country and continuing well into the 1960s.

La Violencia To this day rational discussion of the causes and expressions of *La Violencia* is difficult in Colombia, and a tradition of sectarian historiography and myth-making lives on. According to the Liberals, the Conservative government in Bogotá unleashed a reign of terror, recruiting gunmen, known as *chulavitas*, from the country's most traditional regions to attack Liberal strongholds. Liberal politicians took up arms to defend their people as neighbouring communities fell upon each other, giving rise to the Liberal guerrillas who fought on for years in some areas, particularly the eastern *llanos*.

As far as Conservatives were concerned, the Liberals were bent on denying the legitimacy of the elected government, which was therefore justified in defending itself. Ospina had already taken emergency measures, closing congress and declaring a state of siege in 1949. But it was after Gómez stood down for health reasons in 1953, leaving the government in the hands of one of his ministers, Roberto Urdaneta Arbeláez, an even more sectarian traditionalist, that the government and security forces became instruments of persecution and revenge. Conservative mobs set fire to the buildings of the two great Liberal newspapers, *El Tiempo* and *El Espectador*, and attacked the houses of ex-President López Pumarejo and future Liberal President Carlos Lleras Restrepo.

Atrocity followed atrocity as an undeclared civil war raged across Colombia. Perhaps as many as 300,000 people died in the fighting and massacres of the next ten years - nobody is really sure. In fact, the violence had begun long before the assassination of Gaitán in areas such as the coffee-growing regions of Antioquia and Old Caldas; the political outrage was merely the spark that spread it to other parts and other social groups.

All the ingredients for a social explosion were present in the coffee-growing areas: long-running land disputes within and between small, tightly-knit communities, where rivalries and grievances festered over many generations and had traditionally taken the form of political vendettas.

A Death Foretold

Account by M-19 leader Alvaro Fayad (alias 'El Turco') of the death of his father:

'Soon after the death of Gaitán they murdered my Dad. He lay sprawled on the yellow tiled floor, a thread of blood flowing from his mouth and soaking his white shirt in red. I ran into the kitchen, filled a glass with water and went back into the living room. I knelt down beside him. I wanted to give him a drink, to convince myself that Dad was still alive...

I was about three or four when the Conservatives killed him. I remember that Mum had bought tinned sardines to eat on the journey. That day we were going to leave, once and for all, our home in Ulloa, Valle, where I had been born. We were going into exile, driven out by the violence.

A few minutes before we were due to set out for Cartago, somebody knocked at the door of our house. A man asked if Dad was at home. He said he needed a letter of introduction from him, as he was a leading Valle Liberal politician. Dad came to the door, and as he looked down to take his pen out of his pocket to sign the letter, the man shot him. He fell. The man ran away.

The local Conservative notables arrived soon afterwards. A priest - who is still alive - was with them. They wanted to know if Fayad was good and dead, and shouted that if he was not they would finish him off themselves...

The whole village knew they were going to murder Dad. They talked about his impending death in the cafés, in the streets. But, as in García Márquez's *Crónica de una Muerte Anunciada*, nobody warned him because they thought he already knew...

It was the *pájaros* [Conservative gunmen] who ordered his death: important politicians, the Lozanos, the "Cóndor del Valle"...'

A peculiar feature of the coffee economy exacerbated local tension: the existence of large numbers of seasonal coffee-pickers, landless labourers who travelled from farm to farm during the harvest to supplement the owners' family labour. A large population of rootless people is still a feature of rural

Colombia, and it helps to account for the incredibly rapid growth of coca and poppy cultivation in the empty plains and jungles of eastern and southern Colombia over the past few years.

The armed gangs, whether Conservative *pájaros*, Liberal guerrillas or Communist self-defence *comandantes*, recruited heavily from these unstable elements and increasingly from the growing slums of the big cities, where the trickle of migrants had become a flood as rural depression was followed by sectarian and communal fighting. Small towns such as Ibagué in Tolima became big cities in the space of a few years, as families fled from isolated rural areas, where most of *La Violencia* occurred. Colombia's urban population increased from 39 per cent in 1951 to 52 per cent in 1964.

The years of violence spawned several of the various guerrilla groups which have since become a feature of Colombian political life. The Communist Fuerzas Armadas Revolucionarias de Colombia (FARC) had its origins in the Liberal self-defence guerrillas, while the Castroite Ejército de Liberación Nacional (ELN), the other big armed group still in action today, was a later creation of radicalised middle-class youths dazzled by the Cuban Revolution of 1959. Their icon was Camilo Torres, a young seminarian of good family who despaired of reforming Colombia's tradition-bound society by peaceful means and took to the hills with a handful of followers. He was promptly killed in his first encounter with the army, but the ELN and his legend live on to this day. Other groups such as the Movimiento 19 de Abril (M-19) took up arms later but entered a culture of political violence which had its roots in the 1950s.

The Military Steps In

As the violence spun out of control, leaders of the two parties began to fear for the stability of the country's social and political institutions. Many Conservatives lost confidence in Gómez's ability to keep the situation under control. It was at this point that General Gustavo Rojas Pinilla, the commander of the armed forces, took the almost unheard-of step of carrying out a coup, turning out the Gómez's government and installing a junta of officers. Few tears were shed for the overthrown president.

The Rojas Pinilla régime was a brief and inglorious interlude, which ended in near-farce. But the general set himself the task of 'pacifying' the country while there was still a country left to pacify. He achieved this by a mixture of negotiation and violence, bombing recalcitrant villages but welcoming back into the fold local warlords, particularly from the eastern plains, who proved amenable to persuasion. The result was only partial pacification and, as ever, many innocent casualties.

The traditional parties soon became disillusioned with the general's idiosyncratic rule, which had strong elements of crowd-pleasing populism and threatened their eventual elimination. Exiled leaders from both camps began to negotiate in Spain, to work out a settlement that would make military rule unnecessary and prevent either side from ever resorting to arms again.

This rapprochement produced the 1957 Sitges agreement between ex-Presidents Alberto Lleras Camargo and Laureano Gómez, which set up alternating and power-sharing arrangement known as the National Front. This underpinned political life right through to the late 1970s, and elements of the *modus vivendi* agreed at Sitges still remain in place.

Power Sharing

The National Front, which ran for four presidential terms, until 1974, succeeded in making the country governable again. Rojas Pinilla first had to be disposed of with the minimum of fuss, by means of a 'general strike' by employers and business leaders in May 1957. The framework agreement specified alternating four-year periods of office for Liberal and Conservative presidents. It also involved an equal sharing out of the spoils of office between the parties, to end the political exclusivity that had caused so much violence in the past. But the fact that this solution meant excluding all other political forces guaranteed that other forms of violence would persist.

The formal National Front arrangement ended in 1974. But the understanding that the losing side would be given a share of power lasted until 1986, when Liberal President Virgilio Barco formed a single-party administration. The only time the Conservatives were able to win in a straight fight was when the Liberals divided and opened the door to Belisario Betancur in 1982. But Betancur was far from being a traditional Conservative; much of his political success derived from his ability to present himself as above party, a 'national' candidate who alone could solve the problems that the traditional parties had failed to tackle.

The Constitution of 1991

Betancur's promises turned out to be largely an illusion. When the Liberal former finance minister César Gaviria Trujillo was elected president in 1990 his aim was to modernise the political system. The existing constitution, that of 1886, belonged to a different world, in which the two traditional parties reigned supreme and the president had enormous powers of patronage. There was widespread disillusion, which translated into very high rates of voter abstention, often of 70 per cent or more. There had been a virtually permanent state of siege for decades, during which the executive largely ruled by decree and the military was given wide jurisdiction over security, including trial of civilians by courts martial.

In 1991 a constituent assembly was elected, to draft a new document that would, Gaviria hoped, open up the political system. Symbolically, one of the assembly's three chairmen was Antonio Navarro Wolff, one of the few surviving senior commanders of the M-19 guerrilla organisation and now leader of a legal political party, ADM-19. Colombia's ethnic minorities were also represented for the first time. Debates were wide-ranging and the new constitution, approved in 1991, included some important reforms.

Its main measures were curbs on the powers of the executive and legal guarantees for individuals and minorities. The president would no longer be able to declare an indefinite state of siege and rule by decree for the whole of his term, as many of Gaviria's predecessors had done. Instead, the new constitution contemplated different levels of internal disorder, carefully defined, and placed a limit of nine months during which constitutional guarantees might be suspended. Suspects could only be held for limited times without standing trial; at the same time, the military's right to try civilians for public order offences, widely used and abused during periods of emergency, was curtailed.

All offices were made electable, and the grip of the main parties on the electoral system was loosened. Ethnic minorities were allocated two seats in each house of congress, as of right, and the president could also, if he saw fit, give seats to former guerrillas who agreed to a negotiated 'pacification' deal.

The 1994 Elections

The 1994 elections were the first test for the constitutional reforms. The news was both good and bad. The turnout in the presidential election was much higher than in previous ones, suggesting a reduction in public apathy. The Liberal Ernesto Samper Pizano won a closely-contested poll against the Conservatives' Andrés Pastrana Arango, who just failed to convince voters that he was another Belisario Betancur, a national, above-party figure rather than just the leader of the reformist wing of the Conservative Party.

The two traditional parties retained their grip on congress, demolishing the challenge of the third force, represented by Antonio Navarro Wolff and ADM-19. Navarro's party had split badly after he accepted a seat in Gaviria's cabinet, some former fighters took up their weapons again, and by the time he resigned it was too late to rally his fragmented forces for the presidential campaign.

Other results were less reassuring for the political establishment. The local election results in October 1994 suggested quite widespread disenchantment with the traditional parties. The most remarkable result was in Bogotá, where the 'anti-politician', Antanas Mockus, was elected mayor by a landslide. Similar phenomena were found in Barranquilla, Montería, Cali and other big cities, where non-party or even non-political candidates were swept into power.

The Samper Government

Ernesto Samper Pizano is, in his mid-40s, in the great Colombian tradition of youthful political leaders. He has, nevertheless, been a politician for more than 20 years. He comes from a prominent Bogotá political and professional family and began in public life as head of the Asociación Nacional de Instituciones Financieras (ANIF), the bankers' organisation, where he made a name for himself as something of an iconoclast. His main claim to fame was his campaign for the legalisation of marijuana in the late 1970s, when it was still Colombia's main illicit export and no right-minded person would dream of suggesting such a thing.

Samper's image of youth, energy and ideas carried him into the Casa de Nariño with a comfortable majority over a Conservative rival who, despite or perhaps because of his background as a television presenter (as well as the son of a former president) came across as all image and no substance.

Samper wasted no time in making his presence felt. The suggestion that he, or at least his election campaign, might be involved with drug money, perhaps gave added impetus to his resolve to present an image of reforming zeal, and to differentiate his administration from that of his Liberal predecessor.

He made the running for an international accord against money laundering, which was adopted at the Miami presidential summit in December 1994, arguing that Colombia was not able to tackle a huge international business on its own. In common with other recently-elected Latin American leaders, such as Eduardo Frei in Chile and Rafael Caldera in neighbouring Venezuela, Samper also stressed the need to soften the harsh impact of the free-market economic policies adopted by his predecessor on vulnerable members of society. He even began to talk of an 'alternative model of development', which he suggested would be half-way between free-market capitalism and the discredited state interventionism of the recent past.

But there was no real proposal to reverse or even modify the radically liberal economic policy initiated by his predecessor, César Gaviria. Instead, Samper set out to harness private capital to a far-reaching programme of public investment in services and infrastructure, which he termed the *gran salto social*, or Great Leap Forward for Society. By implication, at least, Samper charged the previous government with neglecting such matters as education, health, housing, efficient utilities, even the impartial administration of justice, in its breakneck dash for economic modernisation and growth based on the free play of market forces.

3 'NARCODEMOCRACY': GUERRILLAS AND DRUGS

The left-wing guerrillas who first appeared in Colombia during *La Violencia* have since become a permanent feature of political life. Some leaders, such as Manuel Marulanda Vélez, the legendary *Tirofijo* (Crackshot), have remained in the field since the late 1940s, surviving successive periods of repression and negotiation. There were rumours in March 1995 that *Tirofijo* had died, perhaps of a heart attack, but there had been many such reports before, and he was still apparently active in September.

In the years following the worst of *La Violencia* guerrilla groups maintained their identity and fighting capability, some remaining resolutely unreconciled out in the hills despite General Rojas Pinilla's efforts to 'pacify' them. But the government knew where they were and their pursuit gave the reconstituted national army something to do. It was such a satisfactory arrangement all round that so-called 'independent republics' run by the left-wing guerrillas, such as Marquetalia and La Uribe, lasted for many years, some of them quite close to the capital.

Successive governments handled this apparently paradoxical situation by declaring a state of siege and keeping it in force for decades at a time. Under its provisions, the military were on a permanent war-footing, which guaranteed higher pay for all and more rapid promotion for the ambitious - on the understanding that their ambitions stopped short of national politics. Instead, senior officers received departmental governorships and control of regional and municipal councils.

As such, political violence was kept within limits that did not threaten the institutional order, and political ambitions were channelled into competition for bureaucratic jobs in which all power groups were assured a share and factions within the traditional parties jockeyed for positions and votes.

President Belisario Betancur, elected in 1982, attempted to complete Rojas Pinilla's partial pacification. Betancur opened a dialogue with the FARC, the ELN, the Maoist Ejército Popular de Liberación (EPL) and the newly-formed M-19 which, again, was partially successful. Some of the many 'fronts' of the FARC agreed to lay down their arms in return for an amnesty and political reforms that would enable them to form legal parties and contest elections.

Yet peace was not to be achieved that simply. The Unión Patriótica (UP) party, formed by former FARC guerrillas, became an easy target for right-wing assassination squads, which were often encouraged by the local political and military authorities. In areas where the UP was elected to local councils, their members were regularly murdered. Massacres became commonplace in the Magdalena Medio, Antioquia and the Urabá region of the Caribbean coast. FARC fronts were re-formed as members defended themselves; in other regions, they had never accepted the Betancur approach and fighting continued. The ELN and EPL likewise remained in the field.

The Drugs Dimension

During the mid-1980s guerrilla and anti-guerrilla violence became tangled up with the growing power of the drug barons, and particularly the so-called Medellín cartel. As leading cocaine traffickers such as Pablo Escobar, Gonzalo Rodríguez Gacha and the Ochoa family prospered, they became substantial landowners with interests to defend against the depredations of the guerrillas in areas like the Magdalena Medio. They found they had much in common with the local military commanders and the 'self-defence' units financed by ranchers and businessmen.

Colombia first became a player in the international drugs business as grower and supplier of marijuana to a booming US market in the 1960s and 1970s, when 'Santa Marta red' was the drug of choice of a whole generation. The crop was grown largely in the Caribbean coast region, particularly the Sierra Nevada de Santa Marta, where *colonos* moved in to plant cannabis on land wrested from Indian groups. The bales of dried leaf were then transported by road to deserted stretches of beach and loaded on to ships for the passage to Florida, Texas or wherever.

During the *marimba* boom Santa Marta was awash with easy money, and the drug-rich *costeños* flaunted their heavy gold bracelets and conspicuous consumption in luxury resort developments such as Rodadero beach. On the lawless Guajira peninsula Cherokee Chieftains with smoked-glass windows cruised the dangerous streets of Riohacha and decent citizens stayed indoors after dark.

The rise of this 'emerging class' was reflected in politics, particularly during the presidency of Julio César Turbay Ayala (1978-82), an archetypal political deal-maker whose supporters were widely believed to have close links to the drug gangs. It was even reflected in popular music: the traditional, African-influenced *cumbia* of the coast, which originated with slavery, was rapidly supplanted by the accordion notes of the *vallenato*, the favourite music of the *mestizo* gunmen and gangsters, *valle-natos* (born in the valley of the Cesar river).

From Marimba to Cocaine

A crackdown by the authorities in both Colombia and the US, together with increasing home-grown production in California and elsewhere, gradually led to the replacement of *marimba* by cocaine, a less bulky, more easily transportable and infinitely more profitable commodity, with a growing market to the north.

Coca leaves, from which cocaine is made, had long been grown in the mountain Indian areas of southern Colombia, largely in the departments of Cauca, Huila and Nariño, where the Páez and Guambiano Indians used it in the ceremonial life of their communities. But when Colombians moved into the cocaine business it was as processors and distributors rather than growers.

International comparative advantage came into play. Conditions for growing coca bushes were just as good, if not better, on the semi-tropical eastern slopes of the Andes further south, in Peru and Bolivia. There was plenty of land and comparatively few people in areas such as the Huallaga and Chapare valleys, which were just being opened up to commercial colonisation. The Colombians, on the other hand, had established transport and supply routes and marketing networks and used these contacts (not to mention their muscle) to forge links with the Bolivian and Peruvian growers.

Poor Peruvian farmers in the Huallaga valley reported that taciturn men with foreign accents and leather satchels bulging with dollars would arrive from nowhere and pay them cash to grow coca bushes. These yielded four harvests a year of small, dull-green leaves, on poor soil and steep slopes, without fertiliser and with minimal cultivation.

Colombian gangs ran fleets of small, unmarked planes, which from the mid-1970s began to ply between the coca-growing regions and the laboratories tucked away in the jungles and hills of southern Colombia. Concealed illegal airstrips proliferated, and initially the leaves were taken to Colombia for processing. But it was not long before the middlemen began to carry out the early stages of manufacture on the spot, converting the coca into PBC (*pasta básica de cocaína*), the raw material of crack, which was much less bulky and could be transported in large quantities in the light aircraft to the Colombian labs for refining into cocaine hydrochloride, the white crystals that found their way, in more or less adulterated form, on to the streets of US cities. For this purpose vast quantities of precursor chemicals were imported from Europe and Brazil, polluting the rivers and water-courses of the Amazon system.

Hundreds of Colombians struggled to get in on the act, but the laws of the jungle and market dictated that the strongest came to dominate, eventually forming loose 'cartels'. The first of these was controlled by Carlos Lehder Rivas, a flamboyant crook who made his first million as a *marimbero*, flying marijuana into Florida. In the mid-1970s he got together with the renegade US financier Robert Vesco to buy his own island, Norman's Cay, in the Bahamas, which he used as a base for shipping cocaine into the US. Lehder set the tone for later cocaine bosses, such as Pablo Escobar, by becoming a local hero and benefactor in his native Armenia, in Quindío. Escobar followed Lehder's lead in other ways: both went into politics for a while (Lehder founded his own neo-fascist party) and both ran right-wing death squads. Lehder was eventually arrested near Medellín in February 1987, extradited to the US and sentenced to 30 years' imprisonment.

'Narco -guerrillas' In the mid-1980s the term 'narcoguerrilla' was first coined, probably by military commander General Gustavo Matamoros, to denote the allegedly close relationship between drug-traffickers and guerrillas in some parts of the country. At first this seemed like pure black propaganda; traffickers were busy organising paramilitary bands to hunt down and kill guerrillas in such areas as the Magdalena Medio, where the so-called MAS (Muerte a Secuestradores or Death to Kidnappers) began its activities in 1981, after a guerrilla unit had kidnapped Nieves Ochoa, daughter of Fabio Ochoa, a leading *capo* of the Medellín cartel.

Military opposition to Betancur's peace initiative was well known, and nothing was more designed to sabotage it than tarring the guerrillas with a *narco* brush. Even those who were prepared to accept that such a relationship existed believed that it was symbiotic: guerrilla units were financing their operations by charging traffickers protection money and buying weapons from them with the money. Later, clear evidence emerged that the relationship was rather closer than that, and that at least some FARC fronts had moved into the drug business on their own account.

Rival cocaine bosses also fought it out between themselves, and at one point Bogotá became a free-fire zone for the warring Medellín and Cali gangs. Differences in operations and approaches between the two leading cartels quickly became apparent. Once leadership of the Medellín interests had fallen into the hands of Pablo Escobar Gaviria a marked psychopathic tendency came to the fore.

Pablo Escobar The evil genius of the Colombian cocaine business was born in Envigado, near Medellín, the son of a schoolteacher who to this day believes he was a saint. He is said to have begun his life of crime by stealing tombstones, chipping off the inscriptions and reselling them. He later graduated to stealing cars, and was arrested for the first time in 1974. By the time he was 19 he was an experienced contract-killer. He then moved into smuggling cocaine by light aircraft to Florida, clearing US$10 million a flight. At the age of 30 he bought the 7,000-acre Hacienda Nápoles in the Magdalena Medio and mounted his first plane over the entrance. As further status symbols he stocked the ranch with a private zoo of exotic animals and bought a car that had belonged to Al Capone.

All drug barons are ruthless by definition, but Escobar imposed his rule by a blood-chilling mix of open-handed populism and murderous vindictiveness. Backed by a private army of hundreds of young killers known as *sicarios*, from the early 1980s he ruled the shanty towns and slums of

Medellín, the *comunas* of the north-eastern and north-western rim of the city, where shacks clinging to the steep hillsides look down on the prosperous districts in the Aburrá valley below. While he was a generous benefactor of the poor, Escobar would brook no opposition. Rival dealers, magistrates, police and politicians were eliminated. The tone for this dark chapter of Colombia's history was set in 1984, when Justice Minister Rodrigo Lara Bonilla was assassinated in his car in the north of Bogotá. He had been rash enough to attempt a crackdown on the burgeoning power of this state-within-a-state.

Pablo Escobar in 1991 (AP)

'Narco -terrorism' This set off the period known as *narcoterrorismo*, when the Medellín organisation confronted the state head on. Escobar was already a considerable power in Medellín, where he used his wealth to build up a large following in the poor suburbs and surrounding towns. He financed low-cost housing, sports stadiums, social centres and thumbed his nose at the stuffy *antioqueño* establishment, who found this flamboyant upstart distasteful. This increased his standing among the dispossessed, and Escobar had himself elected to an alternate seat in the lower house of Congress in 1983.

With judges, generals and politicians bribed or intimidated into silence, Escobar came to believe that he could defeat the Colombian state by force of arms. The more the government tried to crush him, the more ruthlessly he struck back. As the campaign for the 1990 elections got under way, three presidential candidates were gunned down, including the odds-on favourite, Luis Carlos Galán. The security forces, the media and just about everyone else immediately blamed Escobar, despite his strenuous denials. A subsequent judicial investigation instead implicated paramilitary leader Fidel Castaño for two of the killings, and many other atrocities including dozens of massacres and the bombing of an Avianca plane. Castaño, a landowner from Córdoba, on the north coast, was also the brains behind *los Pepes,* a paramilitary unit later created to assist the security forces in tracking down Escobar.

But by then the anti-Escobar movement was unstoppable. While a new presidential candidate, former finance minister César Gaviria, was quickly found to replace Galán, President Virgilio Barco rallied the battered forces of law and order for a full-scale 'war on drugs'. A special anti-narcotics unit was set up within the national police under the command of Colonel Rosso José Serrano, advisers and instructors were brought in from, among others, the British army's Special Air Service (SAS), and close operational relations were developed with the US Drug Enforcement Administration (DEA).

It was a close run thing, but it gradually became clear, even to Escobar, that he could not win a straight fight against the Colombian state. The war was brutal while it lasted: car bombs killed scores in Bogotá, many of them in a failed attempt to assassinate General Miguel Maza Márquez, head of the security police, Departamento Administrativo de Seguridad (DAS), by blowing up its headquarters building in 1990. More than 100 died when an Avianca airliner was blown out of the sky on its way to Medellín. Hundreds of policemen were murdered in that city after Escobar put a bounty on their heads.

But the drug traffickers suffered too. The anti-narcotics police, the so-called Fuerza de Elite, proved highly effective: laboratories were blown up, *sicarios* arrested or killed. The Medellín organisation's most notable loss was the death of Gonzalo Rodríguez Gacha (aka 'El Mexicano') at the hands of the police after he had been on the run for months. Escobar was repeatedly reported to be on the point of falling into the military's hands, but always managed to escape.

Gaviria duly won the 1990 election and adopted a markedly different approach to the Medellín cartel. Unlike Barco, an elderly patrician who felt personally affronted by the brutal pretensions of the cartels, Gaviria was a young and pragmatic technocrat who saw institutional modernisation and economic development as his most urgent priorities. If the peace necessary for his ambitious projects to flourish had to be purchased at a price, then so be it.

The plea-bargaining deals subsequently struck with Escobar and his main henchmen have been the subject of bitter controversy. General Maza Márquez, the former DAS chief, said in November 1994, long after he had retired and had run unsuccessfully for president, that Gaviria became much too close to the Medellín drug bosses, repeatedly sabotaged his efforts to track them down and was over-conciliatory.

Gaviria's supporters deny all this. But the policy did imply considerable concessions. Under legislation passed in 1991, those accused of involvement

Anti-drug police squad   *(Julio Etchart)*

in drug trafficking and of related violent crimes were invited to surrender and confess to at least one offence. If they gave the authorities useful information they were guaranteed lenient sentences. At the same time, legislation against money-laundering and the use of legal fronts for illicit operations was (theoretically) tightened up.

Despite widespread criticism, this approach proved effective. Most important was a provision in the 1991 constitution which ruled out the extradition of Colombian citizens wanted for crimes in other countries. The Medellín bosses were terrified of suffering the same fate as Carlos Lehder, languishing in a US prison. Once that spectre was dispelled, Escobar and his lieutenants calculated that they had nothing to lose by surrendering.

Over the next few months they duly did so and were locked up. But again things were not quite as they seemed. Within a year, in July 1992, Escobar and a dozen other leading retainers coolly walked out of the prison built for them at Envigado, Escobar's home town. In the ensuing uproar, it transpired that Escobar had continued to direct his drug operations with computers, cellular phones, faxes and regular visitors to his luxurious prison quarters.

Heads rolled in the prison service, army and police, as the extent of Escobar's influence over the institutions of the state became clear. A special police-army unit known as the Bloque de Búsqueda was created under General Octavio Vargas Silva to track down and preferably kill Escobar at all costs. It was equipped with the latest electronic intelligence equipment, provided by the US, France and other countries interested in an end to Escobar.

Stung by the appalling damage done to its image both at home and abroad, the Gaviria government gave absolute priority to capturing the fugitive. It took 17 months to achieve, during which time most of his senior associates were killed, captured or surrendered once again.

Escobar was finally shot down by Bloque de Búsqueda agents as he scrambled across the steeply sloping red-tiled roof of a house in a Medellín suburb on 2 December 1993. His habit of keeping in touch with his family by mobile phone had been his undoing; a call to his son that morning had been picked up by police electronic intelligence analysts and passed on to the operational units in Medellín.

Praise was heaped on Gaviria and the Bloque, who were handsomely rewarded for their brilliant achievement. General Vargas Silva was promoted to director of the national police. Only later did it begin to emerge that a high price had again been paid for this public success.

Escobar's organisation was dismantled with help from his bitter Cali rivals, and in return the authorities agreed, tacitly or explicitly, to soft-pedal their operations against the Cali apparatus. One of the Cali organisation's contributions was to finance a shadowy group known as *los Pepes* (People Persecuted by Pablo Escobar), who specialised in arson, assassination and intimidation of Escobar associates.

The Cali Cartel

The Cali cartel, or cartels, were a very different proposition to the crazed gunmen from Medellín. They never appeared to entertain any illusions about winning power by the gun, and preferred to infiltrate Colombia's political and economic institutions while operating behind a façade of business respectability. As they did not seem to threaten the stability of the state, deal-making was preferable to outright warfare.

This is perhaps how the government and security forces rationalised the accommodation they reached with the Cali bosses while Escobar was being hunted down. Apart from a pragmatic desire to use any means to undermine Escobar, the government also knew that the judicial system would have a very difficult job to prove anything against the Cali bosses, of whom the brothers Gilberto and Miguel Rodríguez Orejuela, José Santacruz Londoño and Helmer 'Pacho' Herrera appeared to be the most prominent. They were wanted in the US but for many years there were no charges against them in Colombia - thanks to their infiltration of the judiciary and police, and their lavish use of well-paid lawyers - and the new constitution guaranteed them immunity from extradition.

Washington expected the death of Escobar to be followed by rapid results against the Cali cartel, whom the DEA now blamed for some 80 per cent of the cocaine entering the US market. But US hopes were quickly disappointed, and relations between the two countries grew more and more strained as it became clear that little progress was going to be achieved while Gaviria was in office. The focus for US resentment came to be the chief public prosecutor, Gustavo de Greiff. De Greiff was not a political appointee and he took his independence very seriously. It was his job to apply the law at it stood, and that meant opening contacts with the Cali people, with a view to securing their surrender.

De Greiff finally fell out almost as completely with President Gaviria and his ministers as he had with Janet Reno and US senators such as John Kerrey, who described Colombia as a 'narcodemocracy' in mid-1994. By then US policy-makers were infuriated by De Greiff's apparent failure to make any headway against the organisation they regarded as responsible for bringing demoralisation to US youth and violence to the streets of its cities.

Washington was hoping for better results when the new Liberal President, Ernesto Samper Pizano, took office in early August 1994. But only days after the election results became known a series of audio cassettes mysteriously found their way into the hands of his defeated rival, the Conservative Andrés Pastrana, and thence to the media. The tapes were of conversations between the Rodríguez Orejuela brothers and a journalist, Alberto ('Loco') Giraldo, known for his close contacts with the Cali organisation. In them the brothers appeared to suggest that they had offered millions of dollars to Samper (and Pastrana) campaign funds. Samper angrily denied that he had knowingly received a penny from the drug barons, but suspicions lingered on.

The pressure on Samper intensified when the DEA's long-time resident in Bogotá, Joe Toft, gave a valedictory television interview in which he expressed disillusionment with the lack of progress against the cartels, and repeated the familiar allegations of corruption and 'narcodemocracy'. CNN and *Time* magazine followed with sensational coverage suggesting that Samper was about to do a deal with the Cali cartel, which would involve a nominal punishment in return for legalisation of their business activities.

For months after taking office, Samper struggled to convince the US that he really meant to defeat the Cali organisation. General Octavio Vargas Silva, victor of the war against the Medellín cartel, was one of the first victims. His name had cropped up in the *narcocasetes* as well, and he was brutally snubbed when he went to Washington to visit DEA chief Thomas Constantine and Administration leaders shortly afterwards. Samper nevertheless confirmed him in his post and aroused suspicions in Washington by sending General Rosso Serrano, the DEA's favourite Colombian policeman, off to Washington as embassy police attaché.

But within two months Vargas Silva was out and Serrano, almost universally admired for his honesty and efficiency, was in charge of police headquarters in Bogotá. At the same time, General Camilo Zúñiga was appointed overall commander of the armed forces, and Admiral Holdan Delgado was put in charge of bringing the navy more closely into operations against both drug cartels and guerrillas.

These were significant appointments. After Escobar's elimination, another Bloque de Búsqueda had been set up to target the Cali organisation, under

General Zúñiga, then army commander in Cali and an intelligence expert, and Admiral Delgado. They were energetic in tracking down and destroying laboratories, and developed expertise in tracing and destroying the sophisticated financial and money-laundering networks of the cartels. In March 1995 the authorities made an important breakthrough when they captured José Rodríguez Orejuela, the youngest of the three brothers, and the following month a new public prosecutor, Alfonso Valdivieso Sarmiento, struck at the heart of the ruling Liberal Party by ordering judicial inquiries into the activities of nine leading members suspected of accepting campaign contributions from the cartel.

The decisive blow came in June 1995 when Gilberto Rodríguez Orejuela himself was captured in a nondescript house in northern Cali. The 'military chief' of the cartel, Henry Loaiza, gave himself up a few days later, followed by Víctor Patiño Fómeque, the head of the Cali organisation's shipping operations. On 4 July José (Chepe) Santacruz Londoño, one of the biggest bosses of all, was arrested in a Bogotá restaurant.

The authorities braced themselves for other, smaller 'cartels' to move into the vacuum created by these government successes, but at least it was widely felt, in Colombia and abroad, that Samper had been vindicated, and so had his decision to put Rosso Serrano in charge of the police.

The rosy glow proved short-lived. Continuing investigations by Valdivieso's department suggested not only that the Cali cartel had penetrated every sphere of public life, but that the allegations in the *narcocasetes*, about drug money in the 1994 elections, might have some substance. First the campaign tresurer, Santiago Medina, and then the director, Fernando Botero, were pulled in for questioning, then arrested on suspicion of corruption. Samper continued to deny all knowledge of financial dealings with drug-traffickers, but, in the autumn of 1995, his political future remained uncertain.

The
Long War   During Gaviria's term of office, two big guerrilla organisations agreed to lay down their arms: M-19 and the main body of the EPL, which kept the same initials and called itslf Esperanza, Paz y Libertad (Hope, Peace and Freedom). Two smaller organisations, the Partido Revolucionario de los Trabajadores (PRT) and the Corriente de Renovación Socialista (CRS, a breakaway from the ELN), also took the option of returning to legal political activity.

But negotiations with the two main guerrilla armies, the FARC and the ELN, proved fruitless. Two extended sessions of negotiations were held, in Caracas and the Mexican city of Tlaxcala, in 1992, but without agreement. The main sticking points were the government's demand for the guerrillas to lay down their arms before talks could begin; and the guerrillas' demands

Guerrillas of the CRS fire into the air before surrendering their guns after signing a peace accord with the government *(Ricardo Mazalan/AP)*

for security guarantees for their members which the military found unacceptable.

The underlying problem was that, after so many years of fighting, neither side trusted the other. The guerrillas believed that the military or their paramilitiary auxiliaries would use any truce to murder as many guerrillas as they could find. And they also had the experience of the UP as a warning of what could happen if adequate guarantees were not hammered out before the fighters emerged from the plains and mountains. The military, on the other hand, thought that the guerrillas were only interested in negotiations as a means to regroup their forces and consolidate their hold on parts of the country where they had a strong presence.

Gaviria finally called off the talks in 1992, accusing the guerrillas of lack of commitment. Normal hostilities were resumed. The government was forced to recognise that the guerrillas controlled substantial areas of rural Colombia during the three sets of national elections held in 1994: presidential in February, congressional in June and local in October. The military mobilised thousands of men to maintain order, and voting passed off relatively peacefully in the main urban centres.

But the local elections showed the guerrillas' power in parts of the country, where candidates from the main parties were unable to campaign. The results put mayors and councillors believed to have links with the guerrillas and/or drug traffickers in control of dozens of municipalities, particularly in the coastal cattle-raising departments of Córdoba, Sucre and Cesar.

Samper and the Guerrillas

President Samper's vision was to complete the pacification begun by Betancur and continued, unsuccessfully, by Gaviria. One of his first acts as president was to appoint a high commissioner for peace, Carlos Holmes Trujillo, a seasoned Liberal politician and former minister of education, who was authorised to establish discreet contacts with the guerrilla organisations, sound out public opinion and explore prospects for resuming dialogue.

On 17 November 1994 Samper was able to announce that 'talks about talks' would soon begin, despite a recent upsurge in guerrilla activity. He said he was satisfied that the climate was right for initiating a peace process, though he insisted on the need for 'civil society' to become involved. This meant talks should be discreet but not secret.

The reaction of the FARC, ELN and dissident faction of the EPL was guardedly positive. Mistrust of the military was still deeply ingrained, but Samper's promises to rein in the paramilitaries and the apparent sincerity of his undertaking to improve Colombia's human rights performance promised a decisive break with the Gaviria era.

Subsequent developments were not so encouraging. While the ELN and EPL said they were ready to begin negotiations in mid-1995, provided the government curbed paramilitary death squads, the FARC launched a ferocious new offensive in late May in different parts of the country. Many of Samper's advisers, particularly in the military, felt that the guerrillas had no real interest in peace and were using the talks about talks to gain time. As *Semana* magazine's columnist Roberto Pombo commented, with the guerrillas flush with cocaine dollars, they had little incentive to abandon a lucrative business.

The same publication concluded at the end of September that the dialogue was dead. Two months earlier the military had won a confrontation with Samper over conditions for opening talks with the FARC, which would have involved the complete withdrawal of troops from the region - La Uribe - where negotiations were to take place. The army high command refused point-blank, and Samper was forced to abandon the attempt. Soon afterwards, Holmes Trujillo resigned and was not replced. In August, in the face of a spiral of violence, including several massacres in the Urabá banana-growing region, Samper declared a state of emergency, giving the military additional powers to control outbreaks of violence. At the beginning of October, after the murder of a former vice-presidential candidate at his farm less than 50 miles from Bogotá, the government announced that a new military base would be established at Fusagasugá to confront a build-up of FARC units in the mountainous region west of the capital. Dialogue did indeed appear to be dead.

4   THE ECONOMY: MORE THAN JUST DRUGS

A report by the government statistical department, DANE, in June 1995 showed a surprising development: Colombian exports in the first two months of the year stood at US$1.4 billion (almost 30 per cent up on figures for the same period in 1994). This was in marked contrast to recent trends, which showed a growing trade deficit, and seemed to make nonsense of the recent appreciation of the *peso* - a development which had provoked howls of rage from Colombian exporters, who complained that their goods were becoming uncompetitive in world markets.

The explanation, according to economist Eduardo Sarmiento, is that many of the exports reported were simply fictitious, and were used to justify inflows of capital derived from drug exports.

The foreign trade ministry did not agree, attributing increased revenues to better international prices for traditional exports such as coffee, oil and minerals, and to a dynamic performance by new exports such as coal, flowers and tropical fruits. The exporters' association, Analdex, was not so sure, and promised to go away and analyse the figures.

All of which goes to show that statistics do not always tell the whole story, and this is truer of Colombia than most places.

Coffee Economy

Colombia was an economic backwater in the colonial period, and was held back by a primitive transport system, isolation and insolvency for long periods after independence. By the late 1830s annual exports were still only worth an average of about US$3 million, and 75 per cent of those were of gold, destined mainly for Britain. Most of the population - 1.6 million in 1835 - were engaged in subsistence agriculture.

Tobacco was Colombia's main export for a number of years and was then replaced by quinine. But stagnation only started to give way to rapid development with the growth of coffee cultivation and exports from the 1870s onwards, encouraged by demand in the expanding urban markets of Europe and the US. This was also when the country's first proper bank was formed.

The process known as the *antioqueño* colonisation was launched from the old colonial city of Medellín, founded in 1616. But its secular slumber was not disturbed until, pushed by demographic pressures, settlers began to clear the trees and brush along the western slopes of the Central Cordillera in the early nineteenth century, occupying what is now known as Old Caldas: the present-day departments of Caldas, Risaralda and Quindío. The settlers grew food crops for subsistence to begin with, and later coffee for export.

Until that time gold mining and dredging and diving for pearls in the Aburrá river had been the region's only economic activity. The city of Manizales, which was to become one of the centres of the coffee business, was founded in 1848. Other coffee centres such as Ibagué, Pereira (1863) and Armenia (1889), grew rapidly with the expansion of the industry.

Coffee was the first export crop for which Colombian landowners made big investments in land preparation, technology and infrastructure. Growth really took off from 1910 onwards, although coffee already accounted for about half Colombia's exports by the end of the nineteenth century (by 1924 it was 80 per cent). Production grew from 114,000 bags (60kg) in 1874 to 1 million in 1913 and 5.1 million in 1943.

Big estates were gradually replaced as the main centres of production by family farms established on newly-colonised land in Antioquia and other parts of the Central and Western Cordilleras of the Andes. Coffee growing was too labour-intensive for big estates to be able to compete. By 1904 there were more than 500km of railways, to take the coffee to ports, but Antioquia's take-off really happened after the railway from Medellín down to the Magdalena at Puerto Berrío was completed in 1914. By the mid-1930s the total length of track had quadrupled.

It was a tough business, and from this heroic period derives the *paisas'* countrywide reputation for rugged self-reliance and entrepreneurial acumen. These talents were manifested in the diversification of local capital into new industries in Medellín from the end of the nineteenth century onwards, following the classic import substitution route. Coffee exports gave the initial impetus to manufacturing industry, creating both the capital surplus and the market for the first factories in Medellín in the early years of the twentieth century.

Today there are some 350,000 families involved in coffee-growing in Colombia. Nobody knows exactly how many live off coca and poppy cultivation, but there are probably more of them. The two phenomena are connected: recent poor coffee prices have driven large numbers of growers off the land, not to mention the seasonal pickers who depend on a prosperous coffee sector for employment. Unknown numbers of farmers and pickers have been making their way in recent years from the traditional coffee region of Antioquia and Old Caldas to the boom coca-growing areas in the jungles and plains of eastern and southern Colombia: Guaviare, Vichada, Putumayo and Caquetá.

The coffee industry has been in crisis for some time, a state of affairs that came to a head with a short-lived strike by growers in mid-July 1995. A militant organisation known as the Unidad Cafetera Nacional, supported by some 80 per cent of growers, blocked roads in about 100 districts of the coffee-producing heartland to back up demands for government help with some US$300 million worth of debts the small and medium-sized growers had run up with the banks, and to protest against successive reductions in the price the producers receive for their beans from the Federación Nacional de Cafeteros.

The coffee sector's problems are a combination of fluctuating world prices since the collapse of the International Coffee Agreement in 1989 (they declined sharply in 1995), and *broca* disease, which has affected almost 500,000 hectares, about half of the country's coffee bushes. Producers complain that the lack of money and technical assistance have helped the disease to spread. The government introduced an emergency plan for the coffee sector in May 1995, involving subsidies totalling US$237.5 million, and said it could do nothing more.

Coffee crops before 1989, when they accounted for about 60 per cent of Colombia's export revenues, averaged around 18 million bags. In 1994 the crop was only 11 million, earning 23.75 per cent of Colombia's export income.

Faced with the growing militancy of its own coffee growers and dwindling prices on the world market, the Colombian government joined forces with Central American countries and Brazil in July 1995 to cut exports, in an attempt to stabilise the price. Colombia, the world's biggest producer of mild (arabica) coffee, led the campaign to withhold coffee from the market, arguing that speculators in the consumer countries were driving the price down.

Industrial-isation

Medellín's manufactures provided consumer goods for a growing city, processing the raw materials produced locally or brought in: cotton textiles, foodstuffs, biscuits, brewing and so on. The Bavaria brewery in the town, founded in 1889, became the foundation stone of one of the country's biggest conglomerates: the Grupo Santodomingo. Protective tariffs on textiles, decreed in 1905, helped the process along; Coltejer, Colombia's biggest textile industry, was founded in Medellín in 1907.

Oil was another growth sector, based on Barrancabermeja in the Magdalena Medio, where the US-owned Tropical Oil Co. had its centre of operations. It began exporting in 1926, but on a far smaller scale than in Venezuela, and regulation was far tighter than in the neighbouring country. US capital also flowed into banana production on the Caribbean coast, where a strike took place in 1928 against the United Fruit Company that was immortalised in Gabriel García Márquez' *One Hundred Years of Solitude*.

The Depression abruptly halted the inflow of capital, leading to slower growth but also helping to accelerate the import substitution process, backed by heavy public investment in social overhead projects. Between 1925 and 1953 agricultural production fell from 58.8 per cent of GDP to 36.9 per cent, while industry grew from 7.6 per cent to 17.2 per cent. This process was reflected in the rapid urbanisation of Colombian society. By 1953 almost half the economically-active population were employed outside agriculture, compared with 31.5 per cent in 1925. By then 42.7 per cent of the population lived in towns, and that process was accelerated by social factors, such as land conflicts, which in turn contributed to the climate of violence in the countryside leading to *La Violencia*. These related factors drove increasing numbers of rural people to seek shelter in the cities.

Shopping mall, Medellín   *(Paul Smith)*

Economic Successes Colombia has enjoyed one of the longest uninterrupted periods of economic growth with relative price stability in Latin America, and has a reputation for skilled and efficient economic management. It now has a highly diversified economy, and was the only Latin American country not to suffer a debt crisis during the 1980s, when other governments were defaulting or frantically trying to renegotiate the loans they had accumulated during the petrodollar madness of the preceding decade.

If all goes according to plan, Colombia will become a leading oil exporter before the turn of the century. With a combination of learning from other people's mistakes (particularly those of neighbouring Venezuela) and long experience of successful economic management, Colombia's prospects of using the oil well are quite good.

Economies dominated by single crops tend to become accustomed to handling the booms and busts of fluctuating world commodity markets. Colombian governments have become particularly adept at handling sudden massive inflows of export revenues, followed by equally sudden scarcities.

Unlike Brazil, where inflation became endemic even as the economy was booming, Colombian finance ministers became skilled at neutralising the potentially inflationary effects of such booms; the windfall profits of the coffee boom of the late 1970s was a case in point, and the maintenance of relative price stability since the country became awash with drug money is another.

Colombian governments have traditionally been interventionist: the Conservative administrations of the nineteenth century had a corporatist outlook that involved the protection of monopolies, while the Liberal governments that have dominated the country since the National Front agreement of 1958 have also regulated the economy closely, controlling some basic industries (oil and steel, for example), subsidising prices of consumer goods and exports alike, particularly non-traditional ones, and intervening heavily on the exchange markets to defend the currency and price stability. Import substitution was built on ready access to cheap official credit and high protective tariffs.

This strategy was quite successful for a long time. Colombia maintained a steady growth rate despite the ups and downs of its principal products, and it never had to resort either to heavy borrowing or to the rescheduling of debts that followed in its wake, after the Mexican crisis of 1982.

The Neo-Liberal Turnaround

Change started to come about with the election of César Gaviria in 1990. By that time the free-market wave had swept over the whole continent and Colombia could not remain unaffected. Protectionism was out of fashion, and the high-cost industries fostered by high tariff walls were increasingly uncompetitive.

The solution adopted by Gaviria, a former finance minister, was known as the *revolcón*, a complete turnabout in the direction of economic policy, presided over at the finance ministry by Rudolf Hommes, a US-trained economist. Free trade became the goal, and the country entered into a tariff-cutting arrangement with neighbouring Venezuela that saw trade between the two countries surge from US$600 million in 1991 to almost US$2 billion by 1993.

Together with Venezuela, Colombia signed a free-trade pact with Mexico, forming the so-called Group of Three, which undertook to cut tariffs progressively from 1994. From Colombia's point of view, the Group was a springboard from which eventually to join the North American Free Trade Agreement (NAFTA), formed by the US, Canada and Mexico at the beginning of 1994.

Yet Colombia's liberalising, privatising revolution has been much more cautious and partial than, say, Peru's. This is partly because the directly state-controlled sector in Colombia is much smaller. But there has been no question of selling off the state-owned oil company Ecopetrol, for example, and deregulation of prices and tariffs of public utilities has been slow to come about.

The challenge of an impending oil and gas boom will test the solidity of economic policy again. Already inflows of coca-dollars have helped to strengthen the *peso* and worried exporters who fear being priced out of the market. Samper has promised to maintain gradual devaluation - the so-called 'dirty float' - but may not be able to, and what will happen when petrodollars flood in?

In the first few months of 1995 there were differences of opinion between the government and the autonomous central bank, the Banco de la República, which wanted a strong currency and high interest rates to keep inflation down, while the government also wanted to encourage investment and faster growth. By mid-year it seemed that the year-end inflation rate target of 18 per cent would probably not be met.

But there are also reasonable grounds for optimism. Colombia's economic managers like to compare their policies with those of Chile, the shining example of economic success held up by envious would-be emulators all over Latin America. Finance minister Guillermo Perry Rubio points out that, like Chile, Colombia has never come to depend on short-term foreign capital inflows to balance its budget and finance domestic consumption (unlike Mexico and Argentina), and was in a good position to escape the 'tequila effect' that followed the Mexican *peso* crisis of December 1994.

Steps have already been taken to set up an offshore stabilisation fund, along the lines recommended by the private economic think-tank Fedesarrollo, into which a proportion of oil export revenues are to be paid, to stop the economy becoming too 'dollarised'. And Samper has earmarked large quantities of the expected inflows for social and infrastructural investment.

By the turn of the century the new oilfields of Cusiana-Cupiagua, and the associated Volcanera gas deposits, should make Colombia the second-largest oil producer in Latin America, after Venezuela. The fields, which are being developed by British Petroleum in partnership with Total of France, Triton of the US and Ecopetrol, are in the *piedemonte llanero* in Casanare and Arauca departments, backward and lawless grasslands east of the capital, where the ELN controls large areas of the countryside.

The guerrillas have regularly blown up sections of the existing pipeline from the Caño Limón field in Aruca to the Caribbean port of Coveñas, but this has not stopped BP and its partners from planning to build more.

Drugs and the Economy

Although the impact of drug money on the Colombian economy has been considerable, right from the early days of the marijuana boom in the 1970s, the amounts of money involved, as a percentage of GDP, have probably been much exaggerated. There are plenty of attempts at quantification around, none of them, in the nature of things, much more than an educated guess.

Probably the best of them comes from Francisco Thoumi, an authority on the drug economy at the Universidad de los Andes in Bogotá. He calculates that at least US$1.5-2.5 billion a year has been brought into Colombia every year for the past decade by the drug traffickers. This figure has probably been growing, he thinks, since restrictions on capital movements were lifted in the early 1990s. Other estimates have ranged between US$800 million and US$4 billion of annual inflows.

Even the highest of these estimates only puts these inflows at the equivalent of about five per cent of GDP. Yet that is still a considerable amount: double the income from coffee exports in an average year, or about the same as non-traditional (ie manufactured) exports.

Whether the drug money earnings have been inflationary or not has been a matter of debate. Narcodollars certainly introduce distortions into the economy, leading to a steady appreciation of the *peso* and affecting the activities through which the money is habitually laundered: construction, cattle-ranching and importing of consumer goods. The recent speculative building booms in Cali and San Andrés are ample evidence of the not-always-useful role drug trafficking proceeds play in the Colombian economy.

The
'Informal'
Economy

Like the drug economy, the 'informal' sector is, by its very nature, difficult to measure. But it is known to be important in all third-world countries, even those with strong formal sectors: some 48 per cent of Venezuelans, for example, are thought to work in the informal economy.

Unlicensed factories, street hawkers selling smuggled cigarettes, back-street workshops, all come within the 'informal' economy, which is often closely linked to the 'formal' one of permanently employed workers enjoying paid holidays and social benefits. The historian David Bushnell notes that between 1979 and 1983 industrial employment in Colombia fell sharply for the first time in 50 years, from 517,000 to 472,000. As the formal sector cut back, the informal sector of casual workers and fly-by-night sweatshops correspondingly grew - often because big factories sub-contracted work to them for rock-bottom wages.

The drug economy is, of course, an 'informal' one, with no registered companies or payments of social security contributions. Teenage *sicarios* are aware that they have no job security or prospects, but can make a lot of money in a short time if they are very lucky. There seems to be some connection between the vicissitudes of the textile sector in Medellín and the increase in the number of guns-for-hire.

Much government and international effort has been devoted in recent years to bringing *informales* into the legal economy, often by extending credit to very small businesses on terms that they could not get from the big banks and finance companies. The World Bank recently singled Colombia out as one of the most effective countries in developing sources of private

Street trading   *(Julio Etchart/Reportage)*

credit for *microempresas*. It mentioned Actuar Bogotá, which makes small loans, often of as little as US$100, to groups of 4-5 people with a business idea to create or develop. Similarly, the Inter-American Development Bank has been involved in helping Colombian NGOs to train small farmers, particularly women, to improve their working methods and learn techniques such as reforestation, watershed management, soil conservation and marketing.

Colombia's Conglomerates

Colombia's life has always revolved around urban centres that functioned almost as city states, but the importance of industrial cities such as Medellín, Cali, Barranquilla and Bucaramanga grew rapidly in the post-war years. Some of the great names in Colombian industry and society (Echevarría, Uribe, Ospina, Jaramillo, Restrepo) had their origins in the Spanish colonisation of Antioquia. Since then other regional groups have grown to rival them in importance. Their industrial and financial clout has helped to bring about the growth of the great conglomerates which are such a feature of the Colombian economy.

The two biggest conglomerates are tightly controlled by larger-then-life individuals: Julio Mario Santodomingo and Carlos Ardila Lülle. These two immensely wealthy men are Colombia's sole entries in the *Forbes* magazine annual listing of the world's super-rich. They are locked in combat across the range of their diversified activities.

Julio Mario Santodomingo's group bestrides the Colombian economy, with interests in everything from radio and cellular phones to air transport and natural gas exploration. Santodomingo owns the Avianca airline and Caracol radio network as well as the Bavaria brewery. His empire is probably smaller than the Medellín-based Sindicato Antioqueño, but it is infinitely more influential; it is controlled by one man, whereas the Sindicato is a loose network of mainly medium-sized companies. The group had total sales of US$2.7bn in 1993, the equivalent of almost six per cent of Colombia's GDP. Profits that year amounted to US$200 million.

Santodomingo is a powerful figure but not particularly popular. He unashamedly uses his media interests to promote his business activities and is always ready for a scrap with anyone: he had a well-publicised altercation with *El Tiempo* newspaper, controlled by the Santos family, in 1994. He likes to put his money into politics, too, helping to finance the election campaigns of the main parties impartially. He received something of a setback last year when his offer of money to the campaign of Conservative candidate Andrés Pastrana Arango was rebuffed.

The Carlos Ardila Lülle group, originally based in Bucaramanga, was originally much less diversified than Santodomingo's empire, concentrating on vertical integration of its core drinks business through the acquisition of sugar plantations and refineries, glass-making and bottling plants, cardboard carton manufacturing and distribution networks.

Ardila's first big move out of beverages was when he acquired the Coltejer textile company, the very heart of the old Medellín industrial interests, in the mid-1970s. Ardila also has a chain of radio stations, Radio Cadena Nacional, to rival Santodomingo's Caracol. His organisation had sales of around US$1.4 billion in 1994. Ardila Lülle, 63, exercises direct personal control over his businesses and is much more personally popular than the rather intimidating Santodomingo: in an opinion poll in 1994 32 per cent of respondents picked him out as the person who had done most for Colombia; Santodomingo received that accolade from only 16 per cent.

Drinks Wars

The Colombian drinks industry, the second-largest manufacturing sector in the country, is dominated by these two giants. These are their core activities and nowhere is their rivalry more fierce, especially in the wake of recent liberal policies which have reduced import duties on all forms of beverages (smuggling used to account for a staggering 485,000 cases of whisky each year).

Bavaria is one of the largest companies in South America, formed from the merger in 1968 of Santodomingo's Aguila brewery with the old-established (1889) Bavaria company. Santodomingo is now thought to be the world's fifth-largest brewer, rivalled in South America only by the Brazilian giants Antarctica and Brahma.

Ardila Lülle has seven soft-drink companies, controlling rather more than half the Colombian market. He also has a network of bottling plants and a huge distribution network, based on more than 3,000 trucks.

Until recently it was simple; Santodomingo controlled beer and Ardila Lülle had soft drinks sown up. Coca-Cola and Pepsi Cola are present in Colombia, too, but they are pygmies compared with the two Colombian giants. Now the picture is becoming more complicated. Ardila Lulle has sworn to become Colombia's biggest brewer by the turn of the century, and has poured millions into a new brewing operation at Tocancipá, outside Bogotá, importing equipment from Germany capable of supplying 15 per cent of the Colombian beer market. Santodomingo has retaliated by launching an offensive against Postobón's overwhelming control of soft drinks.

Characteristically, the abrasive Julio Mario got his retaliation in first by launching a bottled beer-and-soft drink mix called Cola y Pola in May 1993. The shandy market had hitherto been dominated by Postobón's Colombiana. It did not work: after an initial, advertising-fuelled sales boom, Cola y Pola sank into obscurity.

Then, in October 1993, Santodomingo launched three new soft drinks, Konga, Wiz and Link, all aimed directly at Postobón products. The products hit the market in a whirlwind of expensive publicity, including an all-star launch concert in Bogotá, with Rubén Blades from Panama topping the bill.

The two giants are also moving into two growth sectors of the beverages market: fruit juices and mineral waters, the expanding markets for which reflect rising living standards and increasing health consciousness among the growing middle class. Santodomingo is ahead of the game in fruit juices, buying the long-established Tutti Frutti company in 1993, and expanding its operations from Medellín to all parts of the country. He then acquired Orense, a producer of fruit juices and jams, in 1994. Finally, Santodomingo launched a new mineral water, Brisa, in mid-1994 to compete with Ardila Lülle's Cristal.

COLOMBIA

Colombia used to be known mainly for its coffee. The beans, which are still grown in the temperate highlands, fuelled the industrial growth of Medellín in the early decades of the 20th century. The business still employs hundreds of thousands of people, but recent price fluctuations have ruined many small growers and there are more alluring ways of making a living from the soil.

Coffee plantations near Quindío
(Tony Morrison/South American Pictures)

Picking ripe berries   (Tony Morrison/South American Pictures)

Cutting poppy heads for milk to make opium (left and below)   (Paul Smith)

Coca and the even more lucrative opium poppies became the favoured crops for go-ahead *campesinos*, with many coffee growers leaving their mountain farms for the lawless plains and jungles of southern Colombia, where coca is the money-spinner. Poppies are grown mainly in the cloud-forests of the *cordilleras*, where upper slopes have been cleared and turned over to the flowers with devastating environmental consequences.

Picking coca leaves
(Mark Read/CAFOD)

Cocaine lab, La Charenta, Caquetá
(Mark Read/CAFOD)

More innocent-looking blooms such as roses and carnations are a recent success story. They are grown under plastic sheeting on the flat *sabana* around Bogotá and air-freighted all over the world - where customs officers have sometimes found small plastic bags of cocaine tucked into the boxes. Tropical fruits - guanábana, chirimoya, pitahaya, granadilla, mango - are also doing well in European supermarkets and are welcomed by government planners as a more respectable alternative to certain other cash-crops.

Cut flower industry (above and right), fruit stall (below)
(Tony Morrison/South American Pictures)

Barrels of oil at a state petroleum process-
ing plant (above) and an engineer at
Ecopetrol refinery (left)
(Nicholas Bright/South American Pictures)

Banana
plantations on
the Caribbean
coast
(Tony
Morrison/South
American
Pictures)

On the Caribbean coast, mainly around
the Gulf of Urabá, bananas are
produced for export to the US and
Europe, where Colombia has the lion's
share of the market. But it is an even
more dangerous game than coca:
hundreds of plantation workers have
been murdered in 1995 as guerrillas and
death squads pursue bloody feuds.

Oil is Colombia's great hope for the
future. The newly-developed Cusiana
and Cupiagua fields in the rolling
grasslands of Casanare will be bringing
in billions of dollars within a few years.
It remains to be seen whether Colombia
will escape the pernicious dependence
on 'black gold' of neighbouring
Venezuela.

5   SOCIETY: RIGHTS UNDER SIEGE

Colombian society is racially quite homogeneous: almost everybody is a *mestizo*, and there are relatively few culturally distinct indigenous and black communities, compared with, say, Bolivia and Peru or Guatemala and Nicaragua. This homogeneity has to some extent been idealised, a fact recognised in the 1991 constitution's assertion of the rights of minority communities to separate representation in congress. Organisations such as Survival International argue forcefully that the rights of the Indian groups such as the Kogi of the Sierra Nevada de Santa Marta and the Guambiano and Páez of the Cauca are still honoured mainly in the breach, and violence against them by *colonos*, settlers from *mestizo* areas, and by the agencies of the state, is widely tolerated.

The Indian communities of Cauca and Huila, some of which have traditionally cultivated coca for ceremonial purposes, have had traumatic experiences with the encroachment of the wider world on their ancestral lands. This is where there has been a rapid expansion of opium poppy cultivation in the past few years, and the Indians have been encouraged to replace their traditional crops with poppies by free distribution of seeds from the intermediaries who buy the latex from the growers.

There have been two main consequences of this development: the clearance of virgin cloud forest to plant poppies has led to devastating erosion over wide areas of the south-central highlands. The seriousness of this ecological disaster was driven home to the local people by a huge landslide in the upper Páez valley in 1993, which wiped out entire Indian communities. The Páez noted bitterly that the national emergency relief system did not appear to be geared to helping them; they complained that such assistance as came was too little and too late.

The other unlooked-for consequence of the Indians' 'integration' into national society has been the close attention of the national police, who launched an eradication campaign against poppy plantations in 1994, including the use of the herbicide glyphosate sprayed from helicopters.

Violence The sentimental image of traditional Colombian rural society, which lingers on in the minds of some conservatives, is that portrayed in the celebrated nineteenth-century novel *María* by Jorge Isaacs, depicting the tranquil life of an *hacienda* in the Cauca valley.

Colombia is now far removed from the unchanging rhythms of that kind of life, but some people still hanker for an imaginary lost world of peace and stability. Among older Colombians there are still some who reminisce about what a paradise the country had been before social and political violence appeared like a malevolent tide and swept away the old Colombia for ever.

High levels of rural violence have been augmented in recent years by an explosion of urban crime, fuelling and feeding off the poverty, unemployment, family breakdown and *anomie* associated with rapid urbanisation all over the third world. Again, Colombia is an extreme case: one in ten of the murders committed anywhere in the world takes place in Colombia, and political and drug-related violence are only a part of it.

A total of 20,000 Colombians met violent deaths in the first eight months of 1995. Colombia's murder rate of 77.5 per 100,000 of population compares with only eight for the US, which is generally regarded as a violent society. Most of the 1995 killings were classified as common crimes by the police, who could expect to solve very few of them.

Human rights

Colombia has an appalling human rights record for a supposedly stable and politically democratic country - a paradox to which organisations such as Amnesty International and Human Rights Watch draw attention. 'Massacre' is a formal category in the compilation of social statistics in Colombia. The NGOs put most of the blame on the armed forces, the police and the 'paramilitary' gangs of armed civilians that have proliferated in many parts of the country in recent years - another long-term legacy of *La Violencia* - sometimes with the active connivance of the military.

The defenders of the paramilitaries claim that they too are a form of 'self-defence' in places where the state cannot, for whatever reason, carry out its obligation to defend the life and property of its citizens. Even the present government, which is committed to social reform and an end to endemic violence, has a certain sympathy with the landowners and cattle-ranchers of the Venezuelan frontier region and the north coast who demand the right to carry arms to protect themselves against the guerrillas preying on their estates and frequently kidnapping them for ransom.

Such claims gloss over the fundamental differences between legitimate small, localised self-

Wounded campesino, attacked by para-militaries during a land dispute
(Julio Etchart/Reportage)

defence groups, which are officially sanctioned, and large paramilitary organisations working closely with the security forces, particularly the army. The majority of the latter operate under the leadership of Fidel Castaño (alias 'Rambo') in central and north-western Colombia, and Victor Carranza in the eastern plains.

The rule of law, while honoured in theory by all Colombian governments, has often been a precarious and limited concept in practice, its interpretation left to local political bosses and military commanders whose interests are not necessarily associated with the impartial administration of justice and honest conduct of affairs. There were well-attested instances in recent years when drug-barons-turned-landowners made common cause with local employers, notables and military commanders to sow terror in conflict-wracked areas such as the Magdalena Medio.

The Samper administration has won some grudging applause from the international human rights organisations and their Colombian counterparts by admitting the problem, accepting responsibility in some cases and promising to do something about it. But, as ever, things are not always as straightforward as they seem.

The apparent absence of the Colombian state from large parts of the country - a phenomenon parodied by García Márquez in his description of Macondo - reflects the weakness and chronic underfunding of local government. Colombia is supposed to be going through a process of decentralisation, with resources and responsibilities for such areas as education and health being transferred from Bogotá to the departmental and municipal levels. But this is a very new idea and it will take a long time for it to catch on - helped along, it is to be hoped, by earmarked resources from oil and gas exports.

The direct election of mayors is a recent innovation; previously they were appointed from Bogotá, along with the departmental governor, and the idea was to keep the central government's finger on the local pulse while placating powerful interests. The priority was not honest and efficient administration but social and political stability. Local governments were almost completely dependent on the centre for their operating resources, and appointments to local administation jobs were equally dependent on the whims and venality of local political bosses.

As a consequence, despite its unusually limited role in national politics, the Colombian military was exceptionally powerful at a local level. Decades of state of siege after *La Violencia* was formally quelled meant that local commanders were granted exceptional powers of administration and were virtually assured of immunity from any retribution for alleged excesses. To try to change this situation is no easy matter.

Little girl on the street in Bogotá   *(Paul Smith)*

No Colombian government could simply admit that the military and their civilian allies are out of control and must be brought to heel. Their role in implementing public policy is too crucial. Hence the emphasis placed by the Samper government on the human rights violations committed by the guerrilla groups - kidnappings, assassinations, the use of *quiebrapatas*, anti-personnel mines in rural areas - and the pressure exerted by the government on the armed groups to agree on norms for the 'humanisation of the war' as a necessary preliminary to peace negotiations.

The government is committed to dealing even-handedly with both guerrilla and right-wing paramilitaries. But meanwhile, armed 'co-operatives' organised and financed by landowners in areas with a high incidence of guerrilla violence are officially permitted in many areas. The gunmen are often the direct descendants of the paramilitary gangs set up with military support in the not-too-distant past as auxiliaries against the guerrillas and drug gangsters.

Human rights organisations claim that about five people a day die in political violence or 'social cleansing', with the security forces and their paramilitary allies responsible for almost three-quarters of the deaths. Street children (*gamines*) are regularly murdered by 'social cleansers', often off-duty policemen paid by shopkeepers and other businesses to clear the streets of beggars, thieves and other undesirables. The Niños de los Andes (Children of the Andes) organisation, set up by a petroleum engineer, Jaime Jaramillo, to help these children, estimates that there are about 5,000 of them sleeping on the streets of Bogotá.

Trade unionists, Indian political leaders, grassroots organisers and left-wing activists have all been victims of the 'death squads'. More than 2,500 members of the Unión Patriótica (UP), the legal political party set up by former FARC guerrillas after they signed a peace agreement in 1984, have since been murdered. They are still dying: on 2 July 1995 two unidentified gumen shot down Luis Espitia, a local UP leader in Chigorodó, in the banana-growing Urabá region. On the previous day another former guerrilla had met an equally violent end: Gustavo Mestre of Esperanza Paz y Libertad (formerly Ejército Popular de Liberación) was shot dead in Turbo, not far away. His murderers may have been FARC gunmen; nobody can be sure. About 700 people died in political violence in Urubá in the first nine months of 1995, as rival armed groups tried to wipe out each others' supporters.

The Sicarios

The most clamorous example of social breakdown spawning appalling social violence is the phenomenon of the teenage *sicario* or assassin, analysed by Alonso Salazar in his influential work on Medellín, *No nacimos pa' semilla*.

The conservatism, with a small and capital c, of *paisa* society was one of the spurs behind Pablo Escobar's increasingly outrageous behaviour: he had himself elected an alternate representative to congress to compete with the local political establishment; he built his own social club when the Club Medellín froze him out even after he had become a very wealthy and successful businessman, with substantial interests in property and land; and he built up his own mass following in the *comunas* and surrounding shanty towns.

Street gang, Medellín
(Paul Smith)

The conversion of Medellín into a violent, drug-riddled urban nightmare was an intense embarrassment to the local establishment. But successive crises in the regional economy, reflecting the ups and downs of both coffee and the textile industry, provided a reservoir of idle and disillusioned youths, often sons of rural immigrants attracted to the city by the prospects of work for them and a good education for their children.

This was the reserve army of nihilistic children from which Escobar recruited the *sicarios*, who spread terror in the later half of the 1980s, assassinating hundreds of policemen during Escobar's war with the state and indulging in violent vendettas as the gangs degenerated into straightforward delinquency after the destruction of the Medellín cartel.

Medellín is still largely Conservative: it is one of the few big cities run by a Conservative administration after the October 1994 local elections. Its mayor, Sergio Naranjo, is also boss of Atlético Nacional, the city's big football team, the Manchester United of Colombia. Both he and it are strongly suspected of links with drug money, ever since Pablo Escobar poured his wealth into the team and built it a new stadium.

Women

The next president of Colombia, in 1998, could easily be a woman. The country has never had a female president, but there is quite a long tradition among the social and political elite of promoting women to senior positions.

The front-runner for the next elections, by a long way, is Noemí Sanín, the former ambassador in London. A Conservative lawyer from Medellín, she has an impressive track record in politics, and was a highly successful foreign minister during the Gaviria administration. Her energetic personal diplomacy is credited with securing Gaviria the secretary-generalship of the Organisation of American States when he left office.

In a May 1995 opinion poll, Sanín beat her rivals, all men, out of sight. These included Andrés Pastrana Arango, the defeated Conservative candidate in the 1994 elections. Her resignation from the London post in August was regarded by some as a betrayal of her old friend, Ernesto Samper, and may have damaged her chances. But she remains a serious possible contender.

Outside the elite, progress for women has been rather slower. The first woman doctor in Colombia graduated in 1925 (after studying abroad), and girls' secondary schools were first required to grant qualifications up to university entrance standard in 1930. In that year married women were also given the same property rights as their husbands.

As far as political rights were concerned, apart from the short-lived initiative by the provincial assembly of Vélez, in eastern Colombia, which granted women the vote in 1853, advances were equally sluggish. Universal male suffrage was not enacted until 1936, and women did not get the vote until the Rojas Pinilla dictatorship of 1953-57. (The general's daughter, María Eugenia, subsequently became a leading politician and stood for president in 1974.)

Only Paraguay in Latin America was slower than Colombia to give women full political rights. Legal divorce was not possible until 1976, and it was not until the 1991 constitution that all marriages, civil and ecclesiastical, could be legally terminated. This same constitution rejected the legalisation of abortion.

Female labour largely powered the development of the Medellín textile industry from the first decade of the twentieth century, much as it did in the Lancashire mills a century earlier. By the mid-1960s women accounted for 15 per cent of the formal workforce, and 30 per cent by 1985. Many were in low-paid and often dangerous jobs, such as tending the flower greenhouses of the Bogotá *sabana*, and many others still went into domestic service. But large numbers also entered the professions, finance and the public administration. Parallel to these developments, the birthrate declined rapidly from around 3.2 per cent a year in the 1960s to 2 per cent by 1980.

Woman in the Firing Line Mónica de Greiff was appointed to the high-profile job of justice minister at the height of President Virgilio Barco's 'war on drugs' in 1989, at the age of 32. She was the fifth justice minister in three years. The assassination of one of her predecessors, Rodrigo Lara Bonilla, in 1984, was one of the opening shots in the Medellín cartel's attempt to intimidate the government into submission.

De Greiff came from a prominent Medellín Liberal family of poets, musicians and lawyers. She followed her father, Gustavo, into the law and had an early blooding in politics, working for the unsuccessful Liberal candidate, Alfonso López Michelsen, in the 1982 presidential election. She became secretary-general of the energy and mines ministry, deputy justice minister and minister in rapid succession during the Barco administration.

She was subjected to death threats almost as soon as she took up the post, and soon decided that the risks for herself and her three-year-old son were too great. She was right to be concerned: four months after her appointment a high court judge in Medellín, Mariela Espinosa Arango, was cut down by a burst of machine-gun fire from a passing car.

She did not, however, disappear from the political scene. When President Ernesto Samper took office in August 1994 he appointed her his principal adviser on international affairs and she was later appointed to the commission charged with privatising Colombian television.

Health, housing and Welfare

President Samper has promised to increase expenditure on social programmes, such as housing, job-creation, health and social welfare from 36.9 per cent to 41.9 per cent of government spending during his four-year term. This is to meet the urgent needs of the 47 per cent of the population whom he regards as living below the poverty line.

In June 1995 the government announced plans to spend US$3 billion on poverty-alleviation programmes to benefit five million children over four years. These included nutrition, health, education and action to reduce violence against children.

Previous presidents have made similar undertakings, without making much of an impact, and scepticism is justifiable. The main targets of this 'great social leap forward' are to create 1.5 million jobs and build 600,000 houses. But the tasks are daunting and achievements in the first year were modest.

The deputy attorney-general, Flavio Rodríguez, complained in May 1995 that 45 per cent of the urban population and 80 per cent in the countryside were unprotected by the public health system. He said the service was underfunded, understaffed, underpaid and in danger of slipping into a coma. He was speaking after a wave of strikes by 75,000 health workers, protesting at government attempts to save money by cutting pay even further: a doctor's pay was to be capped at US$720 a month, or only five times the legal minimum wage; Rodríguez said that 15 years earlier a doctor's salary had been 15 times the minimum.

Partly as a consequence of poor pay prospects, Colombia has the worst health provision in Latin America, with only 1.6 hospital beds per 1,000 inhabitants, compared with a world average of 3.6. Figures compiled by the government's statistical department, DANE, suggest that, of 4.75 million people suffering some form of illness, more than 900,000 receive no medical attention at all, either because it is too expensive or simply not available.

One of Colombia's worst health problems is the lack of clean drinking water in many parts of the country. The ministry of development has concluded that 18 million out of a total population of 34.2 million are without this basic service. These findings contrast with official claims that 76.3 per cent of the urban population have piped water and 19 per cent in rural areas.

The ministry also criticised the quality of drinking water, claiming that only 14 of the 32 departmental capitals had water of satisfactory standard. Minister Rodrigo Marín Bernal, cabinet representative of a coalition of minority ethnic and religious groups, blamed poor management by local governments for many of the problems.

Civil society

President Samper sometimes gives the impression that he is determined to create a 'civil society' in Colombian single-handed. He talks of the need to create a 'social solidarity network' (he has appointed an official, Eduardo Uribe, to co-ordinate it) in which people learn to care for each other and take part in debates on issues with a vital impact on their lives. This is no mean task in a country long innured to very high levels of political and social violence, and accustomed to glaring inequalities between the haves and have-nots.

Grassroots organisations are, in fact, quite thick on the ground in Colombia, from neighbourhood regeneration groups in the poor *comunas* of Medellín to high-powered research institutes or pressure groups such as the Centro de Investigación y Educación Popular (Cinep) and Fedesarrollo. There are also dozens of human, Indian and trade union rights organisations. And the 1991 constitution tried for the first time to give some sense of participation and belonging to religious and ethnic minority groups. But there is no doubt at all that many groups and individuals still feel excluded from society as a whole, and that this is not something that can be put right in one presidential term, however well-intentioned the incumbent.

Nevertheless, Samper has encouraged public debate on issues such as drug-trafficking and the perennial problem of how to 'pacify' the remaining guerrilla armies and bring peace to the countryside. To this end he appointed a 'high commissioner for peace' soon after taking office and gave him the job of sounding out public opinion about the best way of achieving that goal. He resigned in July 1995.

As part of his efforts to improve the country's human rights record, Samper also appointed an ombudsman (*defensor del pueblo*), Jaime Córdoba Triviño, an energetic young lawyer heading a large department of investigators and professionals with the job of ensuring that people's constitutional rights are respected by the authorities. The attorney-general's office also has a special human rights prosecutor, and offices have been set up in military bases to remind soldiers that they are there to protect their fellow citizens, not persecute them.

There is no doubt about Córdoba Triviño's independence and dedication to his task. There is also no doubt about the enormity of it. In March 1995 he produced an annual report to congress that demanded more determined action by the government. He said there were still more than two hundred paramilitary gangs operating in Colombia, and nobody was going to believe in the government's commitment to peace unless these, too, were eliminated.

6   CULTURE: BEYOND MAGICAL REALISM

Colombian life is changing fast, and nowhere more so than in Bogotá. The remote highland capital might have seemed cut off from the rest of the world in the past, but not any more. Blockbuster Video stores, McDonald's restaurants, health clubs for stressed young executives, British-style pubs, Range Rovers, to name but a few, are all heavily advertised symbols of a modern consumer society, to which an increasing number of people have access.

Or consider the vogue for clubs, where thrusting businessmen can take clients for lunch, play squash or simply escape for a while from the frenetic ultra-polluted city just beyond their walls. Two new ones, the Metropolitan Club and Club El Nogal, have recently opened in Bogotá, with no expense spared. Both are aimed at young meritocrats who could not aspire to the traditional social clubs such as the Gun Club or Jockey Club, where a long pedigree is the *sine qua non* for membership. They are not cheap - around US$4,000 for a share - and there are plenty of takers.

Even the urban poor have television sets - eight million for 34 million people - and there are about 2.5 million video recorders in the country. Until the arrival of the US-owned Blockbuster chain this year, most videos on sale were pirated copies, sold from garages in side streets. North American culture has arrived with a vengeance, but must compete with older traditions and tastes.

El Dorado   The pre-Conquest societies of present-day Colombia did not produce great civilisations comparable with the Aztecs and Incas. There were a number of relatively small, autonomous indigenous groups, isolated from each other, which set the pattern of settlement followed after the Conquest.

Nevertheless, the Conquerors found enough gold to whet their appetites and to fuel the legend of El Dorado, focused on Lake Guatavita in the highlands of Boyacá. The Muisca people, who lived around the *Sabana* of Bogotá, were the most skilled craftsmen in gold, and the collection of artifacts in the Banco de la República's Gold Museum in Bogotá is ample evidence of their astonishing ability.

Bogotá at one time liked to be known as the 'Athens of the South', and the seigneurial society depicted in novels such as the nineteenth-century idyll *María* provided the privileged few with the resources and leisure needed to cultivate a highly refined existence. Every *hacendado*, every congressional leader, was also a poet or essayist, and wealthy Colombians liked to keep up to date with developments in the outside world.

Lake Guatavita and the Legend of El Dorado

Though the legend of Eldorado sprouted and multiplied, and expeditions hacked through the jungles of Guiana and Peru in search of a fabulous city of gold, the reality behind it lay here in the highlands of Colombia. Eldorado was not originally a place but a person - *el dorado*, the gilded man. He was the

The raft of El Dorado   *Tony Morrison/South American Pictures*

central figure in a rite performed by the Chibchas here at this sacred lake. It was a kind of coronation ceremony, performed at the appointment of a new *cacique*, or chieftain, to one of the territories of the Chibcha empire. At the shores of the lagoon he was stripped naked, anointed with sticky resin and sprayed with gold dust. A raft of reeds was prepared, with braziers of *moque* incense and piles of gold and jewels on it. The gilded chieftain lay on the raft, and together with four other principal *caciques* he floated out to the centre of the lagoon, to the accompaniment of flutes and drums. When the raft reached the centre, the chieftain dived into the lake, washing off the gold, and all the offerings of gold and jewels were thrown into the water. It isn't clear who or what these offerings were for - whether for a sun god or, as a local Chibcha legend has it, for the spirit of an unfaithful *cacica*, who drowned herself and her love-child in the lake and haunted its depths in the form of a serpent - but, whatever its meaning, the rite itself is historical fact, attested by many Spanish *cronistas* who had the details of Chibcha eye-witnesses...

(from *The Fruit Palace* by Charles Nicholl)

Gabriel García Márquez

The society portrayed by Colombia's most celebrated contemporary writer, Gabriel García Márquez, is equally fantastic, but in a different way: he pioneered and rode to worldwide fame on the boom for Latin American 'magical realism', which reached its apotheosis in *Cien años de soledad* (One Hundred Years of Solitude, 1967), his first big success.

Its dream-like depiction of Colombian coastal society, centred on the imaginary town of Macondo, should perhaps, however, be read as more realistic than magical: he was writing about the world of his childhood, and many of the people, places and incidents depicted are based on fact, or at least on folk memories of real places and happenings. His account of the

1928 Ciénaga banana plantation massacre, for example, is no more far-fetched than any other of that bizarre incident.

García Márquez is no ivory tower aesthete: born in 1928 in the coastal town of Aracataca, the eldest son of the local telegraphist, he was a working journalist for many years, first with *El Universal* of Cartagena, then *El Heraldo* of Barranquilla. He became Paris correspondent of *El Espectador* in 1955. If many of his themes are derived from his early childhood in Aracataca, his style also reflects this early training, in the vividness of the descriptions and the effortless evocation of period and milieu. *El Amor en los tiempos del cólera* (Love in the Time of Cholera, 1985) is a case in point: a recreation of nineteenth-century provincial life in his adopted home of Cartagena de Indias, once the greatest port of the Spanish Main. And his portrait of Simón Bolívar in *El General en su laberinto* (The General in his Labyrinth, 1989), while giving a partisan account of the Liberator's final departure from Bogotá, is a marvellously rounded and convincing recreation.

García Márquez   *(Oswaldo Salas)*

The writer became Colombia's first Nobel Prize winner in 1982 and he is still producing a steady flow of substantial work. The English version of his latest offering, *Del Amor y otros demonios* (Of Love and Others Demons), appeared in June 1995. Its starting point is a story he covered as a junior newspaper reporter in 1949, and it is again set in Cartagena, this time in the eighteenth century, when the city was already past its best.

Despite his predilection for historical exoticism, 'Gabo' has made several (rather unsuccessful) forays into contemporary Colombian politics, and he also became a champion of left-wing governments and causes elsewhere, particularly Cuba and Nicaragua. He was proud to be a friend of Fidel Castro (he was New York correspondent of the Cuban news agency, Prensa Latina, for a brief period) and quarrelled publicly with the outspokenly right-wing (formerly left-wing) Peruvian novelist Mario Vargas Llosa, who stood unsuccessfully for president of his country in 1990.

All of this political activity made him a target for the paramilitary gangs that proliferated in Colombia in the late 1970s and early 1980s and he chose years in exile, in Mexico, France and Spain, before returning in 1982, eventually to settle in Cartagena.

García Márquez was benefactor and guiding spirit of the brilliant but short-lived satirical magazine *Alternativa*, where many of Colombia's most distinguished writers and journalists cut their teeth: Antonio Caballero, Daniel Samper (brother of the current president and editor of the Colombian edition of *Cambio 16*) and Enrique Santos Calderón, now a senior executive of the family newspaper, *El Tiempo*, and very influential political columnist.

Truth and Fiction
García Márquez has been generous towards other Colombian writers, who have perhaps inevitably been overshadowed by his fame. *El General en su laberinto*, for example, is dedicated to his friend Alvaro Mutis 'who presented me with the idea of writing this book'. Mutis has also won international prizes and is another long-time resident of Mexico, but he differs from García Márquez in that he has shunned the local for the universal, to the extent of choosing a recurring main character, Maqroll, with a decidedly un-Colombian name.

Próspero Morales Pradilla, a professor of literature and sociology who died in 1990, achieved great success in the mid-1980s with an erotic historical novel, *Los Pecados de Inés de Hinojosa*, set in his native Tunja in the sixteenth century. It became a best-seller throughout the Spanish-speaking world and was turned into a television series. Just before his death he produced another, *La Mujer doble*, set in eighteenth-century Cartagena. Other interesting contemporary Colombian writers are Manuel Mejía Vallejo, author of *País portátil* (Portable Country), about the guerrillas, Gustavo Alvarez Gardiazábal and Rafael Humberto Moreno-Durán.

Cultural Exports
The harpsichordist Rafael Puyana, the painter and sculptor Fernando Botero and the medical researcher Manuel Elkin Patarroyo have all achieved worldwide recognition in recent years.

Puyana, from a wealthy Bogotá family which made its money from importing wines and spirits, has inevitably made his career abroad, from a base in Paris. The only other internationally-known Colombian classical musician is Carlos Villa, leader of the London Philharmonia in the 1960s, who was personally chosen for the role by Otto Klemperer; he is now with the Philadelphia Orchestra.

Fernando Botero was born into a poor Medellín family in 1932, studied in Madrid, Paris and Florence and moved to New York in 1960. Exhibitions of his paintings, with their characteristically bloated figures of prostitutes, transvestites and Ruritanian generals, have been held all over the world.

More recently, his massive bronze sculptures, many of them produced in Italy, have graced the streets of London, Paris and New York; one of them, which he had donated to his home town, was damaged by a bomb that killed more than 20 people on 10 June 1995. Botero said he wanted the piece left as it was, a monument to the senselessness of political violence.

Like García Márquez, Botero has tended to monopolise the attention of foreign critics. Another Colombian artist who has begun to make an international reputation for himself is Elías Heim, who represented his country at the Venice Biennale in June 1995. He has already received scholarships from the governments of Germany and Israel.

Dr Patarroyo, the oldest of 12 children from a poor farming family from Ataco, in the south of Tolima, has become Colombia's foremost medical researcher, fêted and decorated in the US, France, Sweden and Britain, and widely expected to receive the Nobel Prize one day. As founder and director of the immunology institute of the San Juan de Dios hospital in Bogotá, he developed a vaccine against malaria which has given promising results in trials in Colombia, Tanzania and elsewhere: Colombia's Pacific coast is one of the breeding grounds of cerebral (falsiparous) malaria, the diseases's most deadly form. In a ceremony in May 1995, attended by President Samper, Patarroyo donated his synthetic vaccine SPF66, developed in 1986, to the World Health Organisation.

Music

Colombia has no great classical music tradition, and no purpose-built concert hall to compare with, say, Caracas' magnificent Teresa Carreño centre. But it has a national symphony orchestra, the Orquesta Sinfónica de Colombia, which is supported by the state Colcultura agency, and generally gives its concerts at the Teatro Colón in Bogotá, a theatre which first began staging operas and *zarzuelas* (light operas) in the late nineteenth century.

The Sinfónica is generally held to be inferior artistically to the Orquesta Filarmónica de Bogotá, the Bogotá city government's own band, which has a much better hall to perform in: the León de Greiff salon at the National University. The orchestra has traditionally been as highly politicised as the university itself, recruiting many of its members and artistic directors from the old Soviet Union and Eastern Europe.

Colombia has produced a number of accomplished operatic sopranos, among them Sofía Salazar, Marta Senn, Marina Tafur and Zoraida Salazar. The leading figure in Colombian opera is Gloria Zea, former wife of Fernando Botero, who in 1976 founded the Compañía de Opera de Colombia and the Nueva Opera de Colombia in 1991. A cultural innovator and administrator of singular energy, she also founded the Museo de Arte Moderno in Bogotá in 1970 and was president of Colcultura for eight years (1974-82).

Bogotá also stages a biennial contemporary music festival, at which many leading figures have performed. There is, in addition, a religious music festival in Holy Week in the beautiful colonial city of Popayán.

Musicians at Cartagena   *Julio Etchart/Reportage*

**Folk
Music**
Colombia's folk music and dance are another matter altogether. They are richly varied, reflecting the country's mixture of ethnic and regional influences, and as exciting as the landscapes of the Caribbean, Andes and Amazon. Some 'serious' musicians, such as Daniel Zamudio and José Rozo Contreras, have incorporated folk themes into their compositions.

The black-influenced *cumbias* of the coast, which began with African slaves in Cartagena and Barranquilla, have been all the rage elsewhere in Latin America at different times, as variants of *salsa* (based on the Cuban *son*) are now.

The traditional cumbia ensembles are the *conjunto de cumbia* or the *conjunto de gaitas*. The former is a five-piece band, consisting mainly of percussion, with a small transverse clarinet known as the *pito* playing the melody. The conjunto de gaitas is so called because it has two flutes, one large (the *macho* or male), one small (the *hembra* or female), made from the cactus-like *cardón* plant, as well as percussion and maracas. The gaitas originated with the Indians of the Sierra Nevada de Santa Marta. There is a great gaitas festival every year in San Jacinto, in the coastal department of Bolívar.

But there are also highly commercialised versions of cumbia, developed by the big record companies, with singers such as Leonor González Miña (*la Negra Grande de Colombia*) performing to an accompaniment of saxophones, trumpets and trombones, imitating the big band sound of the great Cuban orchestras of the 1930s.

The other great variety of tropical music in Colombia is the *vallenato*, which originated in coastal Cesar department in the 1940s. The composer Rafael Escalona was responsible for many of the early vallenatos. The form then spread like wildfire across Colombia in the 1970s, reflecting the musical tastes of a new class of free-spending marijuana-linked gangsters, the *marimberos*, who swamped traditional coastal society during that decade.

Although there are several different kinds of vallenato, the thing they all have in common is that they are for singing, not dancing. The words are important, dating from the time when vallenatos were a form of oral dissemination of news and gossip, sung from village to village by roving musicians, rather like the troubadours of medieval Europe. Elements of this topicality linger on: a few years ago there was political deadlock over the naming of a new bridge over the Magdalena at Barranquilla, but the issue was ultimately decided by the dramatic unveiling of a new vallenato song, *Puente Pumarejo*.

The traditional vallenato group consists only of accordion, drum (*caja*) and *guacharaca*, a hollow, ridged tube that is scraped with a stick. The musicians play four different basic rhythms, the slowest of which is the *son* and the fastest the *puya*. In between are the *paseo* and *merengue*.

The great jamboree for lovers of the traditional vallenato is the Festival de la Leyenda Vallenata, which takes place in the main square of Valledupar, capital of Cesar, between 27 and 30 April every year. It is rather like a Welsh eisteddfod, a competition with the emphasis on purity of form and tradition. The groups perform on small raised stages dotted around the square, and the judges pass from one to the other before issuing their verdicts.

Less traditional forms of vallenato also abound, in which the three-piece band is augmented by guitar, amplified bass and percussion. The influence of this tropical music has spread all over Colombia, and can be heard on the radio everywhere.

The same is true of salsa, which originated with Cuban and Puerto Rican exiles in New York but has since taken the entire Hispanic world (and beyond) by storm. If there is a distinctive Colombian form of salsa it is found in Cali, which is a very long way from both the Caribbean and New York. Nevertheless, some of the country's top salsa bands come from there. One theory is that the basic mix for salsa is produced by blending African culture with sugar, as in Cuba, and the Valle del Cauca has both those ingredients in abundance. Grupo Niche, perhaps Cali's best salsa band, gave a sell-out concert in London in July 1995.

Other forms of Colombian folk music and dance still thrive, despite the onslaughts of salsa and vallenato. In the highland areas of central Colombia the most common form is the *bambuco*, which may have been derived from the *currulao* of the Pacific coast sometime in the nineteenth century. It is performed on a variety of stringed instruments based on the Spanish guitar. The instrument par excellence in a bambuco group is the *tiple*, a small 12-string guitar. Two big bambuco festivals are the Mono Núñez, in Ginebra, Valle del Cauca, and the Festival de la Guabina in Vélez, Santander.

Neiva, capital of Huila department, is the home of the *sanjuanero*, staging a festival every year. The *llanos* of eastern Colombia, on the other hand, are similar to neighbouring Venezuela in many ways, including their folk music, which is performed on harps and four-string guitars known as *cuatros*. The characteristic music and dances of the region are the *galerón* and the *joropo*.

Theatre

Colombia has a long-established theatrical tradition, and the biennial festival in Bogotá attracts companies from all over the world. It goes on for two weeks around Holy Week, and was founded in 1981 by the Argentine actress Fanny Mikey, who had earlier formed the Teatro Nacional in 1978. The other Colombian theatre with a world reputation is the Teatro Experimental de Cali, founded by the dramatist Enrique Buenaventura. Fanny Mikey first arrived in Colombia in 1958 to work there. It is generally agreed that its great days are now in the past.

Football

Colombia qualified for the finals of the last two World Cups, when the national team was coached by Francisco Maturana, a (black) dentist from the Chocó. His greatest success was in convincing the players, the Colombian public and many foreign commentators that Colombia was *the* emerging power in world football. The results were mixed and the team's campaign ended in disgrace and death. The new boss of the national team, Hernán Darío Gómez, is a follower of Maturana's super-arrogant, one-touch style.

Big-league football and drug money are inextricably intertwined in Colombia: Pablo Escobar was the benefactor of Atlético Nacional of Medellín and the Rodríguez Orejuela brothers poured their money into América de Cali. Most of the best players, such as Faustino Asprilla, Fredy Rincón and Carlos Valderrama, play in Europe these days.

In the wake of the 1994 World Cup fiasco, the police began investigating the allegations of drug links in depth. By July 1995 they had enough evidence to force Juan José Bellini, president of the Colombian Football Federation, to resign. His name kept on cropping up in documents confiscated from Cali cartel bosses, including José Santacruz Londoño, and Julián Murcillo, the cartel's main front-man and business administrator. Bellini had been first manager and then president of Club Deportivo América in the 1980s, when Miguel Rodríguez Orejuela was on the board.

FURTHER READING AND ADDRESSES

Alape, Arturo, *Tirofijo: Los sueños y las montañas*, Bogotá, 1994

Amnesty International, *Colombia: Political Violence: Myth and Reality*, London, 1994

Archdiocese of Liverpool, Justice & Peace Office, *Por la Vida: Report of an Independent Human Rights Delegation to Colombia*, Liverpool, 1994

Bushnell, David, *The Making of Modern Colombia*, Berkley, 1993

Catholic Institute of International Relations, *Coca, Cocaine and the War on Drugs*, London, 1993

Guzmán Campos, Germán; Fals Borda, Orlando & Umaña Luna, Eduardo, *La Violencia en Colombia*, Bogotá, 1962

International Narcotics Control Board, *Report for 1994*, Vienna, 1995

Lara, Patricia, *Siembra vientos y recogerás tempestades*, Barcelona, 1982

Nicholl, Charles, *The Fruit Palace*, London, 1985

Nieto Arteta, Luis E, *El Café en la sociedad colombiana*, Bogotá, 1981

Ocampo Gaviria, José Antonio *et al*, *Gran enciclopedia de Colombia*, vol 8, *Economía*, Bogotá, 1991. Includes articles by, among others, Miguel Urrutia, Jorge Eduardo Cock, Eduardo Posada Carbó and Salomón Kalmanovitz

Oquist, Paul, *Violencia, conflicto y política en Colombia*, Bogotá, 1978

Pearce, Jenny, *Colombia: Inside the Labyrinth*, London, 1990

Rathbone, John Paul, *Ecuador and Colombia*, London, 1991

Salazar, Alonso, *Born to Die in Medellín*, London, 1992

Sharpless, Richard E, *Gaitán of Colombia*, Pittsburgh, 1978

Smith, Michael L *et al*, *Why People Grow Drugs*, London, 1992

Washington Office on Latin America (WOLA), *The Colombian National Police, Human Rights and US Drug Policy*, Washington DC, 1993

WOLA, *Clear and Present Danger: The US Military and the War on Drugs in the Andes*, Washington DC, 1991

FICTION

García Márquez, Gabriel, *Love in the Time of Cholera*, London, 1988

García Márquez, Gabriel, *One Hundred Years of Solitude*, London, 1970

García Márquez, Gabriel, *The General in His Labyrinth*, London, 1991

Rivera, José Eustacio, *The Vortex*, New York, 1935

ADDRESSES

Children of the Andes,
Enterprise House,
59-65 Upper Ground,
London SE1 9PQ
(NGO working with Colombian street children)

Colombian Committee for Human Rights
Fenner Brockway House,
37-39 Great Guildford Street,
London SE1 0ES

Colombia Human Rights Committee,
PO Box 3130, Washington DC 20010,
USA

Colombian Embassy
3 Hans Crescent
London SW1X 0LR
Tel: 0171-589 9177

Colombian Consulate
140 Park Lane
London W1Y 3AA
Tel: 0171-493 4565

Journey Latin America
14-16 Devonshire Road
London W4 2HD
Tel: 0181-747-3108
(specialist travel agents)

Soliman Travel
113 Earls Court Rd
London SW5 9RL
Tel: 0171-244 6855
(specialising in Colombia)

South American Handbook
(Trade & Travel Publications Ltd)
6 Riverside Court
Lower Bristol Road
Bath BA2 3DZ
Tel: 01225-468141
(best all-round travel guide to Latin America)

Sabor y Salsa
Theberton Street
London N1
Tel: 0171-354-2618
(award-winning Colombian restaurant)

FACTS AND FIGURES

A   GEOGRAPHY

Official name: República de
Colombia
Situation: In northwest corner
of South America between
12°30' and 4°13' N and 66°51'
and 79°71' W. Total land area of
1,138,618 sq km, making it the
fourth-largest country in South
America. It is about the size of
Spain, Portugal and France put
together. Colombia is the only
country with coastlines on both
the Atlantic (1,600km) and
Pacific (1,300km). Its
neighbours are Venezuela and
Brazil to the east, Panama to
the north and Ecuador and Peru
to the south.
Administrative structure: 32
departments and 1,024
municipalities.
Capital: Santa Fe de Bogotá.
Population: 5.7 million (1993).
Other principal cities: Medellín
(2.5 million), Cali (2 million),
Barranquilla (2 million). More
than a third of the population
of 35 million live in these four
cities. Other important centres:
Bucaramanga (750,000),
Cartagena (750,000), Manizales
(500,000), Popayán (250,000),
Cúcuta (600,000), Villavicencio
(300,000). There are a total of
37 cities with a population of
more than 100,000.
Infrastructure: Until quite
recently river transport was the
most practical way of getting
around the country. Also
because of the difficulties of
land communications, air

Colombia
Departments
and Capitals

Administrative Divisions

SANTANDER	Department
ARAUCA	Intendencia
Vichada	Commissariat
D.C.	Capital District
●	Capital

0   150   300 km

services developed early in
Colombia and flying is still the
only way of reaching the almost
uninhabited 50% of the country
that lies to the south and east of
Bogotá and the densely-
populated highlands. Colombia
has about 10,300km of paved
roads, which make up just under
half the total. Main highways
link Bogotá with Medellín via
Manizales; Cali via the Quindío

pass to Ibagué and Armenia;
Bucaramanga via Tunja and on
to Barranquilla and Santa Marta
via the Magdalena valley, or to
Cúcuta and the Venezuelan
frontier (the Pan-American
Highway) to the east. The main
railway line is down the
Magdalena valley from Bogotá
to Santa Marta, but the rail
network is small (3,239km in
1990) and contracting.

International airport at Bogotá (El Dorado), which also has shuttle services (*puente aéreo*) to Medellín and other main cities. National airline: Avianca (owned by the Santodomingo group), which handles both domestic and international flights and also runs the efficient airmail service. Other domestic airlines include SAM and Aces. Main ports are Cartagena, Santa Marta, Barranquilla, Turbo (bananas) and Buenaventura, the only one on the Pacific coast.

Relief and landscape: Colombia is an incredibly varied country, ranging from the Andean highlands to the Caribbean lowlands, the endless grasslands of the Orinoco basin and the Amazon jungle. Most of the population live in the Andean valleys and basins and on the coast. Three mountain ranges run south to north, with deep valleys and basins in between: the Western, Central and Eastern Cordilleras. Five peaks in the Western Cordillera reach 4,000m, and six in the Central Cordillera are more than 5,000m high. Between these two lies the Cauca valley, which runs northwards into the Magdalena, and is one of Colombia's richest agricultural regions. North of Medellín the Central Cordillera, where most of the country's coffee is grown, splits into three ranges which run down to the Caribbean. The Sierra Nevada de Santa Marta is an isolated outcrop rising abruptly from the Caribbean lowlands to dramatic heights, the loftiest being 5,800m. Between the Central and Eastern Cordilleras is the

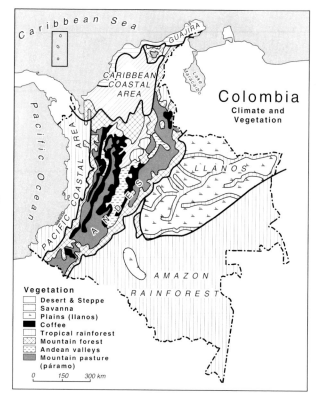

Colombia
Climate and Vegetation

Vegetation
☐ Desert & Steppe
☐ Savanna
☐ Plains (llanos)
■ Coffee
☐ Tropical rainforest
▨ Mountain forest
▨ Andean valleys
▨ Mountain pasture (páramo)

0   150   300 km

Magdalena valley, 1,600km long, flowing into the Caribbean at Barranquilla. Bogotá (2650m) is situated in an intermont basin in the Eastern Cordillera, which eventually splits before entering Venezuela. About 55% of Colombia's surface area is made up of almost deserted grasslands and jungle, with few roads and only 4% of the population. The *llanos* flood for months every year, particularly between June and September.

Temperature and rainfall: Although Colombia is in the tropics and has no real seasons, climate is greatly influenced by altitude: the highlands, where

Bogotá is located, are cool and wet for much of the year, and can get very cold at night. There are permanent snows on the highest peaks of the Central Cordillera and the Sierra Nevada de Santa Marta. The Caribbean coast, the Chocó and the Amazon jungles are hot and wet. Chocó has an annual rainfall of about 400cm and the Amazon region about half that. The Pacific coast is hot and humid, with the temperature never falling below 25C/77F, and rain all year round. There are many lagoons and swampy areas around the mouth of the Magdalena, but further east there is an arid semi-desert in

the Guajira peninsula, on the Venezuelan frontier, with only about 70cm of rainfall a year. The driest months are November-April.
Flora and fauna: The geographical variety of the country is reflected in its plant and animal life. The Caribbean coast has mangrove swamps, palms, scrubland and coral reefs, and the lowlands of the Gulf of Urabá produce bananas and other tropical fruits, while coffee comes mainly from the temperate slopes of the Andean ranges. Higher up, at around 2,000m, there is virgin cloud-forest in such departments as Huila and Cauca, much of which has been cleared in recent years to plant coca and opium poppies. The *páramo* above 2,700m is bare, rough moorland, dotted with cactus-like plants called *frailejones* which can grow to 4m in height. The outcrop of the Sierra de la Macarena, which rises from the southern *llanos* to more than 2,400m, is biodiversity run wild, with a unique variety of plant (4,600 species catalogued) and animal habitats. In the south the grasslands of the *llanos* run into the dense jungles of Caquetá, Putumayo and Amazonas. Jaguars, ocelots and pumas can be found in the jungle, along with two-toed sloths, anteaters and wild boars, coatis and kinkajous and every variety of monkey. Colombia has more species of birds than anywhere else on earth, with more than 1,550 recorded. There are parrots and hummingbirds everywhere; sacred ibis and snowy egrets on the flooded *llanos* and a few condors in the high Andes.

B

POPULATION

Population (1992): 33.4 million. Projection for 2000: 37 million.
Population growth: 1970-80: 2.2%; 1980-92: 1.9%.
Population density (1993): 29.7 inhabitants per sq km.
Urbanisation: 71% (1992).
Age structure: 41% of the pop-ulation are under 18 years of age.
Fertility: The average Colombian woman had 5.3 children in 1970, but only 2.7 in 1992
Birthrate: 24 per 1,000 (1992)
Mortality rate: 6 per 1,000 (1992)
Infant mortality rate: 21 per 1,000 live births (1992; in 1970 the figure was 74)
Average life expectancy: men: 66; women: 72 (both 1992)
Population per doctor: 1,150 (1990)
Adult illiteracy: 13% (1992)
Education: Colombians receive an average of seven years' education. Primary education is theoretically free and compulsory; enrolment rates in

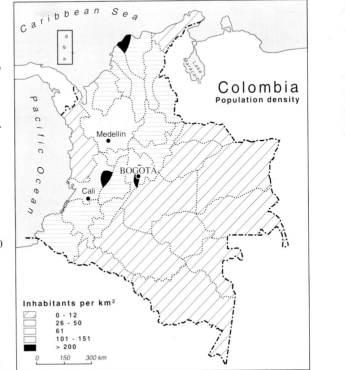

Colombia
Population density

Inhabitants per km²
- 0 - 12
- 26 - 50
- 61
- 101 - 151
- > 200

0   150   300 km

1991 for primary and secondary school stood at 74% and 38% of the school-age population respectively. About 14% go on to higher education. In 1988 there were an estimated 238 institutions of higher education. Social Development Index (UNDP Human Development Index 1994): 50th out of 53 in high group (UK 10th, US 8th), total 173 positions.

Ethnic composition: 60% *mestizo* (mixed Indian-European descent); 20% white; 18% black and mulatto; 2% indigenous Indians.

Language: Spanish, but more than 180 Indian languages and dialects are also spoken, most of them from the Arawak, Carib and Tupi-Guaraní linguistic groups.

Religion: Mainly Roman Catholic, but Protestant evangelicals have gained ground in recent years.

C

HISTORY AND POLITICS

Some key dates * 500: heyday of Tayrona civilisation * 1525: first permanent settlement by Rodrigo de Bastidas at Santa Marta * 1533: Cartagena founded * 1536: Gonzalo Jiménez de Quesada sails up Magdalena, in the same year Sebastián de Benalcázar founds Pasto, Popayán and Cali * 1538: Jiménez de Quesada founds Santa Fe de Bogotá after defeating Muisca inhabitants of Sabana region * 1550: Real Audiencia de Santa Fe set up by Emperor Charles V to administer region * 1564: presidency of Nuevo Reino de Granada created, covering whole of present-day Colombia and Panama, except for Benalcázar's province of Popayán * 1718: viceroyalty created at Bogotá to replace presidency, covering whole of present-day Colombia and Venezuela * 1741: Admiral Vernon attempts unsuccessfully to capture Cartagena * 1794: Antonio Nariño translates *Déclaration des Droits de l'Homme* * 1810: juntas take control of Bogotá, Cali, Cartagena and Socorro * 1812: Bolívar lands at Cartagena * 1816: Spanish General Pablo Morillo's reign of terror in Bogotá * 1819: Bolívar enters Bogotá after defeating the Spanish at Boyacá; Congress of Angostura proclaims Republic of Gran Colombia on 17 December * 1830: Gran Colombia breaks up into component parts * 1849-85: Liberal ascendancy * 1885: Conservatives introduce centralist constitution which lasts until 1991 * 1899-1902: War of Thousand Days * 1903: Panama breaks away * 1948: assassination of Gaitán, *La Violencia* spreads * 1953: coup by General Gustavo Rojas Pinilla * 1957: National Front power-sharing agreement between Liberals and Conservatives which lasts intil 1974 * 1984: Justice Minister Rodrigo Lara Bonilla murdered by hired assassins * 1989: President Barco declares war on drug traffickers after murder of presidential candidate Luis Carlos Galán * 1990: César Gaviria elected president * 1991: new constitution drawn up by constituent assembly * 1993: Pablo Escobar killed by police * 1994: Ernesto Samper elected president.

Constitution: Presidential republic. The 1991 constitution provides for four-year terms with no immediate re-election and direct election of departmental governors. A 102-member senate and 165-seat chamber of representatives, elected in the same year as the president, include designated seats for minority groups such as Indians (two in senate), blacks (two in lower house) and former guerrillas (two in lower house). The constitution also grants autonomy to the central bank (Banco de la República), creates the office of ombudsman (*Defensor del Pueblo*) and replaces the Roman law-based judicial system with an adversarial model with a government prosecution service (*Fiscalía General de la Nación*), whose head is appointed by the Supreme Court.

Head of State: Ernesto Samper Pizano (since 7 August 1994)

Political parties (with seats in senate and chamber of representatives (1994): Partido Liberal (PL, Liberal Party): 56, 88; Partido Social Conservador Colombiano (PSC, Social Conservative Party): 20, 40; independent groups: 24, 33.

Armed forces (1994): 146,400 (including 67,300 conscripts); army 121,000, navy 18,100, air force 7,300. National police total approximately 55,000.

embership of international
ganisations: UN and UN
ganisations; Organisation of
merican States (OAS); Andean
ct; Group of Three; Rio
oup; Association of Caribbean
ates; World Trade
ganisation (GATT)
edia/communications: There
re 75 telephone lines per
1,000 people in 1990. The
main nationally-distributed
newspapers are *El Tiempo* and
El Espectador (Liberal) and *La
Prensa* (Conservative). There
are also important regional
newspapers in Medellín (*El
Colombiano*), Cali (*Occidente*)
and Barranquilla (*El Heraldo*).
The main radio networks are
Caracol, Todelar and RCN. The
state owns the television
channels but lets air time to
private programme-makers. The
most influential TV news
programmes are *CM&* and *QAP*.
The Bogotá weekly news
magazine *Semana* is one of the
best of its kind anywhere in the
world.

ECONOMY

rrency: *peso* ($). The
change rate with the dollar
as 964.5 at end-September
95; 1991: 613.8; 1992:
4.4; 1993: 779.6. Exchange
icy is a 'dirty float', which
ould ensure that the currency
values at more or less the rate
inflation.
flation: 1970-80: 22.3%
80-92: 25.0%; 1993: 22.5%;
94: 22%; 1995 (estimate):
-20%.
oss Domestic Product (GDP):
$48.6bn; average growth rate
70-80: 5.4%; 1980-92: 3.7%;
GDP per capita US$1,330
(1992)
Foreign debt US$17.2bn
(1992); GDP by sector (1992):
agriculture 16%; manufacturing
20%; services 49%
Development aid: US$3.8 per
capita (1991)
Employment by sector (1991):
agriculture 15%, industry 24%,
mining 8%, commerce 6%,
services 47%
Unemployment: (1993): 9.2%
Exports (1994): US$8.4bn, of
which coffee US$1.9bn, oil
US$1.2bn, coal and minerals
US$672m and non-traditional
items (mainly manufactures)
US$4.5bn.
Imports (1993): US$9.8bn, of
which food 9%, fuels 5%, raw
materials 7%, machinery and
transport equipment 33% and
other manufactures 44%.
Principal trading partners
(1992): exports: US (US$2.7bn),
Germany (US$593m), Venezuela
(US$588m), Netherlands
(US$278m); imports: US
(US$2.5bn), Japan (US$494m),
Venezuela (US$438m), Germany
(US$414m).

COLOMBIA AND BRITAIN/UNITED STATES

ade and aid relations with US:
e US has long been Colombia's
ain trading partner, accounting
about 39% of total trade in
92. In FY1995 the Clinton
dministration proposed total aid
Colombia of US$46m, of which
$40m was earmarked for anti-
rcotics operations.

ade and aid relations with the
K: The European Community
counts for about 20% of overall
de. Colombia benefits from the
ecial co-operation agreement
tween the European Union and
Colombia, which since 1989 has
allowed a range of Colombian
goods, including agricultural
products, textiles and other
manufactured goods, into EU
countries without duties or quotas,
as part of the international co-
operation against drug-trafficking.
Britain has recently become the
second-largest foreign investor in
Colombia, with investments worth
US$1.7bn, much of it accounted
for by BP's oil and gas ventures in
the *llanos* east of Bogotá. In FY
1993/94 British bilateral aid to
Colombia totalled £2.4m, of
which almost £900,000 was
specifically 'drug related assistance'.

SOURCES: World Bank, *World
Development Report 1994*; Inter-
American Development Bank,
*Economic and Social Progress in
Latin America*; UNDP, *Human
Development Report 1994*; Europa
Publications, *South America,
Central America and the Caribbean
1995*; Banco de la República;
Departamento Nacional de
Planeación; *South American
Handbook*; Marion Morrison,
Colombia.

BOGOTÁ	capital
■	city 1,000,000 inhabitants
●	500,000 - 1,000,000 inhabitants
●	100,000 - 500,000 inhabitants
•	other towns
---	border
—	main road
—	secondary road
⊨	railway
	canal
	river
	marsh
+	summit
✦	international airport
P	port

0   100 km